Aerial Toys

John F. Hanson

For Dad

Father, mentor, friend

CONTENTS

Acknowledgements

First and foremost, thanks to my father, James B. Hanson, Sr., for helping make the dreams of an aviation-obsessed boy come to life. He always made sure I knew my goals were within reach. Without his constant encouragement and support, none of these events could have taken place.

My mother, Ann, spent many tense hours watching with bitten tongue as I learned the lessons of the air, sometimes the hard way. For simply offering her loving support through the years, I offer my heartfelt thanks. I am very fortunate to have been raised by her.

My brother, Jim, was a constant companion on this adventure in the early years, and he remains a great mentor with whom I still love to talk flying. Thanks for always being there and for being such a good brother, Jim.

Of course, my wife, Peggy, has been an angel about my continuing to spend money on these flying machines like I'm financially hemorrhaging. My daughters, Catherine Sheppard and Christine Cecil all offered encouragement not only in the writing of this book, but also in the author's involvement in what tends to be a very expensive hobby. No one ever complained about the cost, or about the time I spent at the hangar.

Catherine's husband, Ian Sheppard, is a very accomplished photographer, who contributed several photos to chapter 20.

Thanks are also due to Christine's husband, Robby Cecil, whose encyclopedic knowledge of craft beers makes our hangar barbecues complete at the end of the flying day.

Front cover photo courtesy of Sharon Goebel.

Foreword

I once had a dear friend named Steve Swanson in Northfield, Minnesota, who was a retired English professor at St. Olaf College, and also a retired Lutheran minister. He used to really enjoy going for rides in my airplanes, and whenever I would buy a new one the acquisition wasn't really complete until I had taken Steve for a ride. He loved to talk about aviation, and enjoyed the tales I told about buying my first airplane when I was fifteen, and the flying we used to do on the farm when I was a teenager. Steve and I would go for a ride, then end up afterward still talking airplanes. Steve was among other things a published author, and he told me on several occasions that I should be writing all this down. He noted that someday when I'm sitting in a rest home with oatmeal dribbling down the front of my shirt, that it will be too late to pass these memories along. He suggested that a good idea for a book would be an account of each airplane I had owned, in chronological order, telling the story of why I picked each one, a few stories of adventures in them, and what important lessons I learned from each. It sounded like a good idea, and I promised I'd do it.

What can I say about memory? We're all human, and our memories are affected by many things, such as our mood at the time of an event, whether or not we were distracted, preconceptions or prejudices we might have carried to the scene, our mental state of awareness, and so forth. Furthermore, memories of very important events or ones in which we were the hero or the victim, tend to be clearer in our minds. Note that I didn't say more accurate, just that they seem clearer in recall.

Accuracy is another thing altogether. Experts say that if you interview ten witnesses to an event, that you may hear ten different versions of what happened. That may very well be true, and I would add this: if you wait a month to ask them for their accounts, you will get ten accounts that differ a bit more, and if you wait a year or ten years, their accounts will vary enough that they may only vaguely resemble what really happened. Juries in courtrooms are routinely told to take testimony with a grain of salt if the event in question happened decades before.

Some years back, I happened to be the senior captain on a Northwest Airlines Boeing 747-400 that experienced a hard-over rudder. Once we had successfully diverted and landed the crippled airplane, it occurred to me that this was a significant enough event that I was undoubtedly going to be asked to recall and retell the tale many times, some soon and some at much later dates. I decided, for all of the above reasons, that it would be wise to sit down at a computer once the adrenalin wore off and write an account of what happened as completely and accurately as I could. I did, and it was four pages of single spaced narrative. After careful proofreading to make sure it was as accurate as possible, I pronounced it done. I printed it out, and let that master copy be my reference for answering all future questions. I'm very glad I did, because as I told the story, no matter how hard I fought the tendency, the facts seemed to change a tiny bit each time I told it. The only way I could be absolutely sure the story remained factual in its retelling was to go back to that document and reread it before every interview. Each time I did that, I'd always find something to scratch my head about: "Wow, did it really happen that way? I'm not sure I recall that..." But though the years may dull or warp the memory, the black and white printout that I wrote of the event three days after the incident doesn't lie.

Having said all of the above, it occurred to me that Steve Swanson was exactly right. Time is indeed of the essence. It's time to put these memories down while I can still do it and have them be relatively accurate. My personal pilot logbook was of great value in details and timing. Had it not been for the FAA mandated recordkeeping I had to keep in that log, the task of remembering the dates I bought and sold the various planes, their registration numbers, and significant trips or events taken with them would have been impossible. The walk back through the pages of my logbooks has been fun. As I read the entries, the memories, faded though some of them are, came rushing back. My life in the air is in those logs, and I've tried to bring to life here the magic carpets that carried me on those adventures: the airplanes themselves, best described as my toys aloft.

My apologies to any reader who recalls any of the events differently, but as I said, memory is a very individual thing. All I can promise is that I have not consciously embellished anything. What follows is the story of all the planes I have owned, as accurately as I can recall, how I came to choose them, and the experiences I had with them. I've promised myself to resist the temptation to change this account substantially as the years pass - the younger I am when I write this, the more accurate will be the memories!

The whole project has been a case of "easier said than done," as the saying goes. I started the project at Steve's suggestion, and it went slowly at first. But the more I wrote the easier it became, and finally here it is. Steve passed away before I finished, and never got to see the finished project. I feel very bad about that. Although he wasn't a licensed pilot, he was one of my all time favorite copilots. I'm not the writer he was, but I think he would have enjoyed seeing the results of his prodding.

Let's go back to my childhood and talk flying.

An Obsessed Youngster

One of the first toys I remember from my childhood was a little red airplane, made of rubber. It had one open cockpit, in which Mickey Mouse performed the pilot duties. I spent hours with that plane and one other, a metal model of a P-47, making engine noises with my mouth and shooting landing after landing on the living room floor. My mother used to gently remove them from my bed after I had fallen asleep.

One thing led to another, and as the years passed I graduated to model airplanes, both plastic and balsa wood. I used to stay up late putting them together, and would be peeling dried glue off my fingers the next day.

I remember two things about having my tonsils out in the hospital: when they put the ether mask on me, I heard a sound like washing machines; and when I woke after the operation my father had a big blue and yellow model of a Piper Cub Special for me. If he was trying to take my mind off the sore throat, it worked! And, of course, all the doctor-prescribed ice cream didn't hurt...

Over the next ten years, I built and flew uncounted control line planes, the ones where you start a small gas engine by flipping the prop. The many small cuts and nicks inflicted when you couldn't get your fingers out of the way fast enough were worn like Stephen Crane's Red Badge of Courage at school the next day. I recall the thrill of being spoken to by one of the cute girls in class when she saw the bandages on my right hand and asked about the injury. Trying to keep my 12-year-old cool and doing my best Roscoe Turner imitation, I replied with one word: "propeller." Unfortunately, she wasn't impressed, and I remained a single man until I was well into my twenties.

Once I got the engine going and ran 30' to where the control lines were fastened to a handle, a friend would launch the plane for me. As the pilot, I stood at the center of a 60' circle and rotated around and around while the plane flew the circumference. I made it go up and down by simply tilting the handle, and I could do lots of tricks with it, including loops and wingovers. It was loads of fun, and made me so dizzy I couldn't stand up, as the plane carried several minutes of fuel!

The next natural step in the progression was Radio Control airplanes, and I built and flew many of those. They were expensive, but I saved my allowance and got some help at birthdays and Christmas to acquire all that equipment. I had many fun flights controlling a model from several hundred feet away. Today they'd call them UAVs or drones, but then they were just fun. They would be controllable up to about a quarter mile, which is where the radio range tapered off. I had to be careful, though, as they moved along at a pretty good clip, and if I got them downwind and let my attention lapse, they could shrink to a tiny dot in the sky and then disappear altogether. They were usually painted a bright color, though, and I was careful to have a little label with my name address, phone number, and the word REWARD doped to the fuselage to be read by the Good Samaritan who would find it in his yard.

The one time I inadvertently tested that system, though, it didn't work as planned. I had a beautiful little high wing model, and went to a neighboring farmers field to fly it. I was having a great time, but lost sight of the plane at one point. Unfortunately, it had about half its fuel remaining and about 100' of altitude when it decided to go off on its own, and there was nothing I could do but put head downwind to look for it. I never found it. I went back several times over the space of a week, looking in different places each time, but it remained a mystery. Sometimes even now when I think of that day, I recall my last glimpse of the plane. It's somehow fun to think it's still up there, flying around, free at last.

My brother Jim would join me occasionally, and I have a very vivid memory of him and me flying my Falcon 56 RC plane in a field not too far from home, chosen for its vast openness, with only one big oak tree right in the middle. We guided the little plane back and forth, diving for speed as it crossed the field, with the little gas engine screaming at high pitch. The inevitable happened, of course, and I'll never forget the immediate transition from high pitched roar to total silence when the plane flew right into center of that lone oak tree at full speed. Total silence. The engine alone flew out of the far side of the tree, as the wings, fuselage, and tail fluttered separately down from the tree to the turf beneath. Undaunted, I repaired the plane as best I could, but it never flew quite the same again.

My father, Jim Hanson, was ex-Navy-WWII, a Pearl Harbor survivor, who spent the post war years first as a contractor, then an airline pilot. He was a very senior pilot for North Central Airlines, and always had a lot of energy. He couldn't sit still for long, and loved to build houses, so we moved a lot, always from one house he had recently built into the next of his creations. I recall a wide variety of homes and schools, and actually attended seven different elementary schools. The mental roster of nonfamily childhood friends I had starts at middle school, as that is where the schools stopped changing, although the seemingly never ending series of houses did not. The constants in my early years were thus family and my love for aviation. I knew from day one that I was destined to be a pilot.

In the early 1960s, my father traded one of the houses for a 160 acre farm just south of Ann Arbor, Michigan, which he farmed on his time off from his "day job" as a pilot for North Central Airlines. He knew that I wanted more than anything to own a real airplane, so when I was about 14 and started talking to him about how we could make it happen, he was a wonderful encouraging mentor. When he bought that farm, which had room for an airstrip, all the ingredients were there. All I had to do was figure out how to buy a plane, put it on the farm strip, and the rest would take care of itself. Well, maybe not quite *take care of itself*, but at least become a possibility. That's where my dad's advice and assistance came in.

I can't recall whether it was my father's idea or mine, but in a flash of entrepreneurial inspiration I bought eleven baby pigs and raised them in one of the barns we had. I sold them for enough money to buy my first plane. The plan worked really well (raising pigs is extremely profitable when your father lets you use a barn for free, and buys all the feed). Dad also began keeping his ear to the ground at work, looking for inexpensive planes that might be good for me. I, of course, began researching specific airplane types that would fit my purpose: small two place planes that would make good trainers and could also be operated out of an 800' farm airstrip.

At that point, World War Two had been over for about 18 years, and the used airplane market was full of types that were products of the post war personal aircraft production boom. Small airports everywhere were covered with Piper Cubs, Cessna 120s and 140s, Taylorcrafts, Aeroncas, Ercoupes, Luscombes, and many more. They were almost all two-seat planes, perfect for learning to fly, and then for use as fun personal transport machines. The post-WWII examples were all less than twenty years old, although there were also a sizable number of pre-War examples still flying at that time.

I bought and then devoured every magazine I could find that described the characteristics of each type. I'm sure my father got tired of my endless questions about each one. There were several that stood out from the rest, and it appeared to me that I should probably be looking for a Piper Cub, Aeronca Champ, or Taylorcraft.

One day Dad came home with a hot lead. One of his friends, another North Central Airlines captain, had a 1947 Taylorcraft BC-12D for sale. It was flyable, but had sat outside in a severe hailstorm in Minot, North Dakota and needed refurbishment. The price was only $550! I bought it sight unseen. The die was cast, and I then owned the first in what was to become a long line of dream machines.

Airplane #1: 1947 Taylorcraft BC-12D NC44091

This was the first airplane I actually owned. I bought it from an airline pilot named John Chambers, and for the $550 sale price he delivered the airplane from Minot, North Dakota to Ann Arbor, Michigan. My teenage excitement could hardly be contained as I awaited its arrival, and when word finally came that it had arrived at Ann Arbor Airport, I could not wait to see it. I'll never forget the feeling when I first set eyes on my very own airplane! It was a cool cloudy day, a bit breezy, and my first glimpse of my sleek ship was from the old airport administration office on State Road at Ann Arbor Airport. From a distance it was undeniably a Taylorcraft, a fabric covered ship with two place side-by-side seating. It was powered by a Continental 65hp engine, and had a wood prop. It was covered with duct tape, which had been applied over the hail damage in the wings, and had a metal plate over a huge hole in the windshield. That must have been quite a hailstorm! The plane needed much TLC, but I was up for it. My enthusiasm blinded me to the work that lay ahead, and I was so excited I couldn't sleep for weeks.

The first step was to get the plane home to the farm, where I could work on it. Dad had walked the area on the farm where he thought the strip should go, and deemed it suitable for landing the Taylorcraft. On the appointed day, my older brother, Jim, drove us to the airport to get the plane, as I was only 15 at the time, and didn't yet have my driver's license. I watched as Dad propped the engine to get it started (no starter or even electrical system!), and taxied out to the runway and took off. We stayed and watched as he went around the traffic pattern and landed it once to check the plane out and get a feel for it before landing on the short farm strip. When he took off again and headed south, we raced home to watch him land on the farm. We got there in time to see him make a few low passes over the strip, and finally land the plane. It was home! I was now not just an actual airplane owner, but I tied it down on the lawn right outside my bedroom window. I thought I was in heaven.

JAN 1964

I recall one cold winter day when I went outside and just sat in the plane, imagining what it would be like when I refurbished it and could actually fly in it. It had a battery powered low frequency radio in it, and I remember putting on an old headset that came with the plane and turned it on. I sat on that cold day and turned the tuning knob, listening for anything. I expected to hear Clark Gable saying "China Clipper, calling Alameda, come in Alameda..." or some such thing, but all I could hear was static. Oh well, I knew I'd eventually hear the China Clipper over that radio, it would just have to wait until I had the plane done. Magic.

Next step: dismantle the plane and get it into the shop on the farm. Dad had helped me prepare one stall of the three-car garage as the airplane factory. It was a separately walled in unit, and had an old oil burning stove in it, so I could work in the cold Michigan Winter. It was by no means modern furnace technology, and it took forever to heat the shop once I got it going. After a couple of hours or so, the heat soaked the walls and floor, and the shop stayed toasty warm. Now 50 years later, I can still close my eyes and smell the old fashioned scent of that old oil stove.

JAN 1964

With the wings, engine, and tail feathers removed, the fuselage fit nicely in the shop, and I removed the fabric covering and started to strip the old primer from the frame using emery cloth. My father guided me through the steps, and without his help I'd have truly been at a loss. His history of working with light planes at all stages of disrepair over the years was invaluable.

Of course, when you work on an actual licensed aircraft, there are rules that must be followed. The FAA has strict standards that must be met, and Dad watched me closely, offering help and advice where needed. When it came time to have the plane inspected by an FAA rated mechanic, my father brought in a friend from the airline, a jovial fellow named Lee Koepke, who was a master North Central Airlines mechanic in Detroit. The project was still in the early stages when Lee first came and looked, and I recall being quite nervous about it until Lee pronounced the basic fuselage frame as sound. He told me to proceed, and he'd return as needed at the various stages. Before the newly bare metal had a chance to rust, I then primed the bare steel of the fuselage frame with bright yellow zinc chromate primer, and began to think about the next step.

Winter turned to spring, and my enthusiasm for the project took a hit. It was easy to head into the heated shop and work and dream when the snow was flying, but forcing myself in there when the weather outside was warm was a different story entirely. Besides, my sixteenth birthday had come and gone, and I was of a legal age to fly an airplane solo. My thoughts turned from rebuilding my airplane to swapping the project for a flyable plane. Again, my father entered with an idea.

Airplane #2: 1945 Aeronca 7AC Champ N82052

Dad knew me pretty well, and when he saw my enthusiasm for the shop project begin to wane, he again put his ear to the ground. Through his network of airline friends, he found another plane for me. Several of his airline pilot buddies had recently completed rebuilding a 1945 Aeronca 7AC, a perfect plane for me to start my actual flying lessons. The price was right, and so I sold the Taylorcraft project in pieces, and put my savings with the proceeds. The Aeronca was also in the upper Midwest (Minneapolis), but getting it back to the farm just south of Ann Arbor was no problem. Dad rode a

North Central jump seat from Detroit to Minneapolis, picked up the plane, and flew it back for me. I was left to wait for my new acquisition, and I didn't sleep too well in the meantime.

My father had kept in touch on the ferry flight, and given me a rough idea of when he'd be arriving with the Champ. I kept my eyes and ears trained on the sky from my second-floor bedroom at the farm all day, and my vigilance was rewarded when dad buzzed the house with my new plane. I can still hear the sound of the 65hp Continental engine as it roared by a hundred feet above the roof, and the sight of the plane climbing as it passed. Dad landed the plane on the same strip of land where he had landed the Taylorcraft. At last, my own flyable plane, and a nice one at that!

As long as I kept that plane on the farm, we tied it down outside my bedroom window, and the last thing I'd do before bed, regardless of weather, was to go outside and check the tie down ropes to make sure they were secure. In lieu of actual in-the-ground tie down anchors, we simply strategically positioned several heavy farm implements and tied the plane to those. The picture above shows the Champ nestled safely next to the barn, securely tied to a field disc, a full size tractor, and for good measure a small garden tractor on the tail. By golly, that Champ wasn't going anywhere!

The first thing I would do upon waking in the morning was to lift the shade in my bedroom and make sure the Champ had made it through the night safely. It always did.

Now all I needed was an instructor. My father declined to teach me himself, thinking he'd be too cautious. It was probably a good call, as I didn't care to be the only pilot with 1,000 hours of dual instruction before being allowed to solo... Another good friend of my father, Dick Downs, offered to do the instructing. Dick was the Detroit base Chief Pilot for North Central Airlines. He was a military pilot in WWII, flying "the Hump" in DC-3s. He was also a good instructor, obviously fearless, as he regularly climbed into a small plane with a 16 year old kid who inadvertently scared the dickens out of him!

Having my own plane tied outside the kitchen door, where I could see it at any time simply by glancing out my bedroom window, was magical. I would go out whenever I had a few spare moments, and tinker with it, cleaning off dirt or readjusting seat belts. One Spring day, I got into the cockpit and sat in the front seat, just watching clouds roll in from the southwest. I sat there imagining what it might be like to encounter a thunderstorm while actually flying, when rain started to spatter on the windshield in front of me. The storm was moving in fast, and as the drops intensified, I thought for a moment about making a dash for the house, but then thought better of it. I stayed right where I was, with the Champ tied securely to the ground, and watched and listened to the storm pass from the safety of the front seat. The rain was very loud as it landed on the fabric covering of the plane, punctuated by lightning and thunder right outside, and water ran in streams down the windshield 2 feet in front of my face. I will always carry with me those sights, sounds and smells of my first rainstorm encountered while alone in an airplane. Yes, it was tied down on the lawn right outside my house, but to me I was flying through a storm, guiding the ship with my own hands. Again, magic.

The farm airstrip was small, approximately 800 feet long, and was not an ideal place from which to stage my lessons, so we moved the plane to Ann Arbor Municipal Airport for the duration of my first lessons. Dick would meet me there, and we then had the luxury of a long paved runway, 6/24. We also had the option of using a shorter (but more forgiving) gravel one, 13/31. The airport, of course, is still there, as is runway 6/24. The gravel runway has long since disappeared, replaced by a newer turf runway, 12/30 a bit further to the west on the airport.

The lessons with Dick went well. I progressed rapidly, due to my intense motivation (I could think of little else). All of my exposure to aviation through my father, including flying with him in the many planes he owned himself during my youth, gave me a good foundation on which to build during my time with Dick. It all came quickly and naturally to me, and after 9 hours of logged dual instruction, on April 28, 1964 we taxied to the departure end of runway 13 at Ann Arbor. I recall the engine ticking over patiently as Dick got out of the rear seat. He smiled and said, "shoot 3 landings, and come back here and pick me up."

My heart was pounding as I lined the Champ up with the old gravel runway and opened the throttle. Without the weight of the instructor, the little 65hp Aeronca seemed to leap into the air. I will never forget the feeling of nervous elation as I climbed away, my fate now totally in my own hands. Dick was right, the plane performed better with just me in it, and I quickly arrived at pattern altitude on downwind. The Champ had no electrical system or radios, and of course Ann Arbor had no control tower in those days, so I was not bothered by having to handle radio communications. It was just me and my plane, going around the pattern doing what I loved, doing what I had dreamed of for so long.

The 3 landings over, I taxied back to pick up Dick. He congratulated me, and offered a critique of my performance: good job, although I ended up a bit high (quite high, actually) on my last approach. A forward slip resulted in a nice touchdown at the normal point on the runway, though, and he said "nice recovery," a phrase I would hear repeatedly over the years in a variety of airplanes. Later, on the airline, I heard that many times from copilots who would diplomatically say "nice recovery" when I would salvage a poor approach for a reasonably smooth touchdown. It was much better to hear than what they really wanted to say: "Well, you old fart, I wouldn't have given a snowball's chance in Hell for you to pull that one out, but by golly you did it..."

The standard action on completing one's first solo is to cut off the fledgling airman's shirttail, and the instructor signs it with the date on it. I'm sure we did that, but I have searched for the souvenir repeatedly in the years since and can't find it. It got lost in one of my many moves over time. I'd give anything to have it now, but it's gone.

The first solo milestone now past, I moved on under the able guidance of Dick Downs to master the various items on the Private Pilot training checklist. When I had checked all the squares, I had to fulfill the last experience requirements: operation at airports with control towers, as well as some basic instrument flying skills. As the Champ had no radio or flight instruments, I had to rent an airplane that was suitably equipped. I also had to take the FAA Private Pilot check ride in a radio-equipped airplane, so we decided to do it all at once. I found a Cessna 150 locally that I could rent, but I had to use their instructors for insurance purposes, so I checked that last square with two different instructors, Lance Gordon and Barry Brablec. Then, since the radio was also required for the Private Pilot check ride, I continued to rent it for that ride. I studied fiercely for it, reviewing all the material on which I'd already been tested on the FAA Private Pilot written exam. The check ride was a nonevent, so it all paid off.

I took the ride on May 4, 1965 with Stew Peet, an FAA designated examiner. Stew became a good friend over the years, as he had a perfect personality for the instructing and check ride role. Later, as a flight instructor myself during college, I sent many prospective pilots to Stew for their check rides. I always felt good putting them in his hands for their final look before going off on their own.

I continued to keep the plane at Ann Arbor for a while, since I had gotten used to the field. Ann Arbor Municipal was on my way home from high school, so I always swung by to check on the plane, flying it when weather allowed. I had formed a great relationship with Mary Rosasco (later Mary Tinker), the lady who ran the airport administration office. If the weather was not good enough to fly, she always made me feel welcome if I stopped to just chat and have a Coke. My Champ was tied down right outside her office window, and if I ever had a bad feeling about heavy weather moving in, all I had to do was call Mary from wherever I was, home, school, etc., and she'd run out and check my tie down ropes. It was very comforting to hear her voice come back on the phone and say, "I checked her, John, and the ropes are good." She understood exactly what I was feeling all the time. I always called her my "second mother," even to her face. She's gone now, and as I look back on all the folks I've known in my flying experiences, I'll always put her near the top of the list of my favorite people. Rest in peace, Mary, and thanks.

It wasn't long before I gained the experience and skill necessary to operate out of an 800' farm strip, and I eventually moved the Champ back home, where I could again check the tie down ropes before bed, and say good morning to the plane simply by looking out the bedroom window. Those were golden times. I found myself forgoing many of the activities at high school such as sports, just so I could fly after school. I recall on one occasion the gym class teacher specifically timed my fifty-yard dash, and asked why I wasn't on the track team. I answered with a question:

"Well, the team practices after school, don't they?"
He looked at me curiously. "Of course," he said.
"Well, that's my time to fly."
"Huh?"
"You know, fly. Like with a plane?"

"Oh, well, suit yourself. But I know you will 'Letter' if you go out for the team."

"Thanks, but I'd rather fly."

"It's up to you…"

Yes, I knew it was up to me, that's why I chose to fly!

I knew nothing lasts forever, and the world was full of airplanes. So when I came to the decision that it was time to move the Champ along, my father's connections again came in handy. My dad passed along my thoughts about trading airplanes to one of his good friends, another North Central Airlines captain, Bill Barber. Bill was hired in my dad's pilot class in 1952 at Wisconsin Central Airlines, the forerunner of North Central. Bill knew a ticket agent for United Airlines who wanted to learn to fly, and told him "Go look at John's airplane. It's a good one. Buy it." So the next thing I knew, this fellow was at our door on the farm, identifying himself as a friend of Bill's. He pointed at the Champ tied down on the lawn a hundred feet away, and said "Is that the plane you have for sale?" I indicated it was, and he said, "I'll take it." Ohmigosh, I thought, he never even walked around it! I didn't argue, and soon cash changed hands and the Champ flew away. I would say, "never to be seen again," but that wouldn't be accurate, as we shall see.

Airplane #3: 1946 Taylorcraft N5249M

My first instructor, Dick Downs, was interested not just in flying airplanes, but also in rebuilding them. He had been involved in restoring a 1946 Taylorcraft BC-12D with a friend of his, Tom Hill. This lovely airplane was just being completed as the Champ left the farm, and we soon reached agreement on a price. Eleven days after my last flight in the Champ, the shiny like new red Taylorcraft was tied down on the lawn outside my bedroom window in the recently vacated space.

I was especially excited to own a finer example of the same type of plane as my rough first ship. There was something about not having completed the restoration on my first plane before selling it that made this acquisition particularly satisfying. I now had a chance to do some Taylorcraft flying that I denied myself by selling the first one before it was done.

The Taylorcraft was designed by C. G. Taylor, one of the designers of the forerunner of the Piper Cub. Early airplane designers in the 1920s and 1930s felt that a light plane should be capable of aerobatics. The Taylorcraft was certified for simple aerobatics, and my father was of the opinion that I should be exposed to this capability of my plane. So it was that one day when dad and I went flying in the Taylorcraft, he told me he wanted to show me something, and checked to make sure our seat belts were fastened as we climbed to altitude. The next thing I knew he was diving for speed, and we were soon pulling G's as he entered a loop. I'll never forget the excited feeling as we went over the top and came out the bottom. The Taylorcraft gas tank is mounted in the fuselage, directly in front of the windshield, and the filler cap is about two feet in front of your face. As we went over the top, dad must have wanted to hang there upside down for a few seconds, because we were momentarily weightless and a small amount of gas streamed out of the tank and spread across the windshield. For a few seconds the pungent aroma of gasoline filled the cockpit. They say the sense of smell is very closely connected to memories, and I believe it - today I can easily recall the feeling of my first loop with dad whenever I smell raw gasoline.

A few spins and a wingover or two later, we headed for the farm. He made me swear I wouldn't try those things until I had gained some more experience and gotten some actual aerobatic instruction, but it was exciting to know I now owned a plane that was even capable of such stunts.

A Taylorcraft is a great plane for a small farm strip, as it has a big lightly loaded wing with a high lift airfoil. Even with only 65 horsepower, it got off the ground nicely with two adults aboard, and landed in the same space quite well, as long as the speed was under control. If you came in a bit too fast, though, the little plane liked to float and float. It didn't want to quit flying and settle onto the hay until it was good and ready. I learned this lesson the hard way one warm August day. After a short flight, I returned to the strip and obviously was not slow enough as I crossed the runway threshold. I concentrated on holding the plane a foot off the ground as it slowed, and by the time it was ready to settle on the turf I had used most of the already-short runway. There is a split second in that situation where you are faced with the decision to proceed with the landing or go around, and I quickly weighed the two possible outcomes: either proceed with the landing and probably run into the mature August corn off the end at a fairly slow speed; or attempt a go around and perhaps catch the top of the corn with the landing gear as I tried to climb away at slow speed.

Thinking quickly, I didn't like either scenario, but I recall thinking hitting seven-foot tall corn with the mains on the ground and the plane under control was the better of the two choices available to me, and in an instant that's the option I chose. For good measure, I added about half throttle as I entered the corn, hoping the prop blast on the tail would keep me from flipping on my back. I entered the corn doing what felt like 1,000 mph but in reality was probably around 20 mph. The prop blast on the tail worked, and the tail stayed down. The arresting cable on a US Navy aircraft carrier has nothing on August Michigan corn, as I stopped in approximately one airplane length. Lots of noise, a quick stop, and all was quiet save for the quiet patient idling of the 65hp Continental. The adrenaline was pumping, and my heart was beating fast as I shut the engine down and got out to see if I had done any damage to my pride and joy.

My father had been out doing something on the tractor, and had watched the whole drama. I looked down the airstrip and saw him coming in my direction as fast as the tractor would go. He looked at me, then at the airplane, and quickly determined that no serious damage had been done. He offered to help me push the plane back onto the strip and turn it around. He said if I got in, he'd prop the engine for me so I could taxi back to the parking spot, where I could clean the plane up and look it over carefully for any damage.

Anyone with even a casual familiarity with farming knows how much milk there is in even one ear of mature corn, and I was astounded to see my lovely Taylorcraft covered with proof of that. The rapidly turning propeller had pulverized any ears it encountered, and sprayed the results over what seemed like the entire plane. It was a terrible gooey mess, but I got the hose and lovingly and contritely washed off the evidence of my inexperience. It took an hour, but the plane was once again as clean as a whistle. By that time my father had finished his chores and returned with the tractor, and walked around the plane with me, looking for scratches and dents. We were both pleased to find that the only damage was to my pride. After a long talk about the importance of speed control on landing accuracy, he smiled and said to go have fun.

One side note is in order about how the timing of random acts can affect your life in unforeseen ways. All summer, knowing how short the strip was, we had been discussing the possibility of a runway excursion of exactly this type. We finally decided to do something about lessening the danger, and my brother, Jim, and I had removed the fence from the end of the airstrip the week previous to my incident. Little did I know as we sweated while removing the obstacle, that I would blast right through the same space just one week later with my plane! To this day, I'm grateful for the timing of that fence removal!

One of the many fun activities in which you may engage with a private plane is called a "breakfast flight." They are a planned event at a small airport, wherein the local aviation enthusiasts or flying clubs designate a specific Saturday or Sunday morning as a breakfast flight, or "pancake breakfast," and publicize it all over the region. They usually open for business at 7am, at which time everyone who is free within 100 miles or so gets in their plane and flies to the breakfast at that airport. There are planes parked everywhere, and it's always great fun to have the standard fare of pancakes, sausage, eggs, juice, and coffee, then walk around amongst the planes. If the weather is good and the event is well publicized, it is common to have upwards of 100 planes show up for one of these events. My father thought it would be a good time to introduce me to the idea of pancakes mixed with aviation, and he suggested that he and I get in my Taylorcraft and fly to a nearby pancake breakfast for that weekend, which happened to be at the Mt. Pleasant, Michigan airport. Sounded like fun to me, so bright and early Sunday morning, we were off.

It's hard to describe the activity level of a fly in breakfast. There are airplanes everywhere in the traffic pattern and on the ground. A neophyte like me would have turned tail and run from that beehive, but Dad slipped us in there as slick as anything, and soon we were walking around sightseeing after breakfast. We were lazily watching planes approach and land, mentally grading the pilots on their technique, when my father said urgently, "Gear up! His gear is up!" I followed his gaze and saw a Mooney 21, a retractable gear four-place airplane, just starting his landing flare. It looked normal except for the landing gear, which was still retracted. He had obviously simply forgotten to extend it in the excitement of the crowded traffic pattern. It was a helpless feeling, standing there and watching it happen, as there was nothing we could do. He leveled off, and soon settled onto the runway on the plane's belly. The prop instantly stopped, of course, and the ship slid to a stop in the center of the runway in short order. The door opened, and a very embarrassed pilot stepped out on the wing. The traffic pattern was still full, however, and planes soon began to execute missed approaches. The onlookers mobilized quickly, and about 40-50 able-bodied enthusiasts simply ran out from the grass, picked up the airplane so the gear could be extended, and removed it from the runway. The whole thing took only several minutes, and the fly in was soon back in business. I'm sure that pilot never forgot to extend the gear again.

My brother had also been excited about learning to fly, and the Taylorcraft was ideal for that purpose. Dick Downs was again pressed into service, and the Taylorcraft moved to Ann Arbor Airport for the long roomy runways a student needs, and soon Jim had also soloed.

Airplane #4: Aeronca Champ N82052 (Again...)

As the Champ had flown away, I sadly watched it go, never expecting to see it again. As luck would have it, though, the fellow who bought it had encountered some bad luck with the engine. The 65hp Continental had quit (stuff happens...), and he had glided down and landed without harm in a farmer's field. He replaced the engine with another used one, an engine with less time since overhaul (65hp Continentals were "a dime a dozen" in the mid '60s, I wish I had bought 100 of them and pickled and stored them...). The experience had made him wary, though, and he reconsidered his desire to learn to fly. Word got back to me through the grapevine that the plane was again for sale. I loved that plane, and gave him a call. I was pleased to find that his asking price with the new engine was actually less than he had paid me for the plane not too many months previous. By this time, I had sold the Taylorcraft, so the timing was good. Soon, by May of 1965, I once again owned my beloved Champ. Just about to graduate from high school, and I had owned three airplanes (four if you count owning the Champ twice...).

Of course, an airplane as basic as the Champ will let you build time in your logbook, but it is not equipped sufficiently to gain your advanced pilot ratings. Enter my mentor (dad) once again. My father had always known my desire to be a professional pilot, and as I gained experience, my resolve only intensified. Aware of the equipment requirement for both my brother and me to advance, he purchased a suitable airplane from the local Cessna dealer. It was a blue 1961 Cessna 180, N6497X, an ex-Michigan State Police airplane (you could still faintly see where they had painted over the police shield on the door). I really got serious in that plane, under the guidance and instruction of Dick Downs and Barry Brablec, and took my Commercial Pilot check ride in it from Stew Peet on June 15, 1966. Dick Downs then dove into my instrument flying with me, and on July 11, 1966 I received my instrument rating from Stew Peet in N6497X. I soon added to my advanced ratings in the Cessna 180 with Certified Flight Instructor ratings.

With the 180 in the stable, I had no need to keep the Champ, so for the second time I sold it. I watched it fly away, this time for good. I sold it to a flying club in Indiana, and felt good about it going to a group of aviators who would fly it regularly. Many years later, I tried to track it down in the FAA aircraft registry, thinking that if I could buy it and rebuild it, it would be a fun plane to own. How many pilots can boast being able to go out and fly the same plane in which they first soloed? I was successful in finding the last registered owner (no longer the flying club), who told me that the plane had been involved in an accident in which someone was killed. It was never rebuilt.

That saddened me greatly, and I abandoned that dream. I prefer now to always think of N82052 as it looked when I saw it out the window of my bedroom on the farm, waiting patiently for me to come fly.

Thank you, my little Aeronca Champ, for all the fun, and all you taught me. Rest in peace.

I was soon introduced to another lovely airplane, a Cessna 120, N2386N. I won't include it in my list, as I didn't actually own it. My father had purchased it mainly for my brother to fly, as he was also interested in building time towards an eventual airline career. I did spend many hours in it, both recreationally and as Jim's instructor.

My instructing and charter activities at Twining Aviation kept me so busy with flying that I did not see the need for owning my own airplane for a while. In April of 1968, I was offered a position in a pilot class at North Central Airlines. I was twenty years old, and just completing my junior year at the University of Michigan, but flying for the airlines had always been my goal, so I jumped at the chance. I flew for the summer of 1968 as a first officer on Convair 440s, and was promptly furloughed by the airline in September.

It had been a magical summer, but now as a man of forced leisure I simply returned to the university and registered for fall classes as if I had never left (indeed, I had never even told them I was leaving, I just quietly left at the end of my junior year to go be an airline pilot...). I could then, as a senior, attend school with a completely different attitude. I had the all important airline seniority number in my pocket, so I could take my last year of Aerospace Engineering courses without the distraction of having to be a flight instructor in my spare time. This carried the risk of the airline calling me back to active service before I graduated, but I decided to take that risk. It was a good gamble, as I completed my senior year at the University of Michigan still on furlough, and North Central called me back to active duty two weeks after graduation in the spring.

Airplane #5: Cessna 120

This airplane appears on the list because I did own it, although I kept it for such a short time that I do not even have the N# in my records. This was a Cessna 120 that I bought from a fellow North Central Airlines pilot. He told me it had a fresh engine overhaul, and was a great airplane. I went and looked at it in Wisconsin, and when I arrived, it was dark and raining, so I couldn't fly it. But it looked good under the hangar lights with the rain beating on the tin roof, and what the heck it did have a fresh engine overhaul (although by an individual mechanic, not an actual engine shop...), and the seller was a friend, so I bought it. I was about to learn a lesson about buying planes...

I returned later on a sunny day to bring the plane home to Ann Arbor. I paid for the plane and flew it back. It flew fine, but the engine oil pressure was "acting funny'" so I had a local shop that I trusted inspect it. The verdict was swift: the "overhaul" had been done in a very slipshod unprofessional manner, and several shortcuts had been taken. I contacted the mechanic who did the overhaul, and told him that my local mechanic would contact the FAA about the deficiencies in the overhaul, unless someone made it right. The Wisconsin mechanic, after some light persuading, humbly offered to pay me what I had given for the plane, after which it was his and he could do whatever he wanted with it. I got my money back and signed the plane over to him. He came with his pickup truck and tools and got the engine, took it back home and (I guess) re-overhauled it, brought it back, put it back on the plane, and flew it away. As Shakespeare said, All's Well That Ends Well, but that was one plane I wasn't sorry to see go. Lesson learned: don't buy a plane without flying it first, unless of course it's a project plane, bought for the purpose of restoring it yourself.

Airplane #6: 1946 Cessna 120 N2896N

Living the dream I had long sought, I satisfied my flying needs wearing an airline uniform. It wasn't until September 1976 that I again felt the desire to have a plane of my own, and the opportunity came when I saw a Cessna 120, N2896N, for sale. I was quite familiar with the small Cessna type, as I had extensively flown the 120 my father had purchased for us several years previous, and I was delighted to find this new one. It was soon mine.

Most of my long single engine cross countries had been in aircraft I had flown on charters for Twining Aviation, and with N2896N I determined to stretch my legs and take some long trips. By this time I had been married and divorced once, and I remained very good friends with Marilyn Molbreak, my ex-wife. She enjoyed flying in the 120, and we decided to take a couple of trips in it. In December 1976 we went to Fort Lauderdale and back, to see the countryside and visit my parents, who by then lived in Ft. Lauderdale, Florida.

In September 1977 Marilyn and I took N2896N to Colorado to visit her sister, and I experienced first hand exactly how anemic a fully loaded 85hp Cessna 120 could be. The mile high airports were right at the takeoff performance limit of the little Cessna 120, so I carefully chose the airport at Denver that gave the longest runways: Denver Stapleton International. I'm sure we got some funny looks from the terminal building as we taxied amongst the big iron, but I didn't care how we looked - we had 12,000-foot runways available for our use. I have a very vivid memory of taking off on one of those 12,000 foot runways, and only having about 50' altitude over the far end!

Having provided many hours of enjoyable flying, N2896N left my life in May 1978. I was about to answeri a call from a part of aviation I had only slightly experienced: open cockpits.

Airplane #7: 1941 Ryan ST3-KR N53998

The first ride in an open cockpit airplane that I can actually recall was in a Fairchild PT-23. This was a low wing monoplane with two open cockpits, designed and manufactured specifically for training WWII pilots. It was made largely of wood, and was covered with fabric. Powered by a 220hp Continental radial engine, it was a noisy but fun airplane. It was an honest, good flying ship, as were all the planes ever produced by Fairchild. I remember that ride as a completely different kind of flying, a whole new world, one I knew I had to enter.

Once I decided to search for an open cockpit airplane, I found that the plane that was most readily available was a Ryan PT-22, a different animal altogether than a Fairchild PT-23. I found N53998 for sale in an aviation ad publication called Trade-A-Plane, and gave the fellow a call. I went to Holland, Michigan, to see the plane, and instantly fell in love (with the plane, not the guy...). The first time I set eyes on the Ryan, it was sitting in the sun outside its hangar. My heart beat faster at the possibility of flying the Michigan skies in an open cockpit airplane, and a quick demo ride in the ship confirmed my desire to buy it. A short time later, we agreed on a price, and the plane was soon mine.

After arranging for the necessary funds, I returned for a quick checkout before bringing the plane home to Ann Arbor. I climbed in the back cockpit, the seller climbed in the front, and we left to fly around the pattern a few times. I'm sure I must have given the poor guy a few frights as I struggled with flying a WWII trainer while being distracted by the windy open cockpit. I was also definitely not used to landing a tail dragger with a radial engine, since you fly it from the rear cockpit and forward visibility virtually disappears in the landing flare. Suffice it to say that the seller was only too happy to get out after the first and only trip around the traffic pattern, especially considering that we came to rest after several screeching swerves. I had much to learn about how to steer a radial engine airplane after the runway disappears behind that big engine.

"You'll be fine," the seller said over his shoulder as he climbed off the wing. I taxied back and took off for Ann Arbor, in command of my very own open cockpit Ryan!

The trip home was wonderful. The engine was exquisitely loud, and I even got the chance to circumnavigate a few thundershowers. I smiled as I picked my way between the cumuli, the wind howling around my leather helmet. Now THIS was flying...

I finally owned a plane worthy of admiring stares at any airport. I seized the chance to fly it whenever the weather permitted. Of course, weather was now more of a concern, especially in the northern part of the United States. While it was technically possible to fly it year round, any temps below about 45 degrees were just plain uncomfortable, making it a three season airplane in Michigan. Not to worry, I had more fun in three seasons with that plane than I ever could have in four with any closed cockpit plane I'd ever owned!

The engine on the Ryan was a Kinner R-56, a 160 hp radial. With only five cylinders, it had a very distinctive popping sound, not unlike an antique John Deere tractor, which earned the PT-22 the nickname "Maytag Messerschmitt." Several of my previous planes needed to be started by hand propping, so I was no stranger to that, but the Ryan also needed to be propped, and with the radial and its massive wooden prop, hand propping took on a whole new dimension. As you pulled the prop through by hand, it stopped in 5 different positions every two revolutions. The crankshaft was much higher than on the planes I was used to propping, and only two of those 5 positions gave appropriate leverage in starting, so the procedure for starting the Kinner was involved.

First, as is true with any radial engine, if the plane sits overnight (or longer), oil tends to run past the rings into the combustion chambers of the lower cylinders. This oil can be purged by carefully and slowly pulling the prop through at least two (more is better) full revolutions with the magnetos off and mixture in idle cutoff, feeling for liquid lock as the lower cylinders pass through their compression stroke. Unless you strategically place rags or a drip pan under the engine, the oil will drain out of the exhaust pipes onto the hangar floor. If it feels like the prop hits something "solid," you have a liquid lock, which must be fixed before going further – starting the engine in this condition will quickly ruin it. Pulling the spark plugs in the lower cylinders will allow the oil to drain, solving the problem, and this was a common procedure with my Ryan.

After being assured there is no oil in the lower cylinders, the next step is to actually start it. Ideally someone you trust must hold the brakes and handle the cockpit controls. I often did this procedure alone, but it is definitely NOT preferable, and even with the tail tied down with a stout rope, one must be VERY careful, as many people have been severely injured or killed hand propping airplanes. One must remember that when I owned this plane, it was a different era, and starting an engine by hand was much more common than it is today. Hand starting one alone today is frowned upon, not only by the

FAA but also all aviation insurance companies, for good reason. End of disclaimer.

The engine had to be manually primed, while pulling it through by hand. When the prop was in either of the two positions allowing proper leverage, the magnetos were switched on, and with great care the prop, now "hot," could be pulled, and with any luck the engine would start. It goes without saying that you are in extremely close proximity to a now-turning prop, driven by a running 160hp radial engine. One doesn't hang around, but rather learns to quickly retreat. It reminds me of the printed instructions I once saw on a package of Chinese firecrackers, which economically advised, "Place on ground. Light fuse. Retire quickly." That's it in a nutshell. Hand propping is a young man's game. Exhilarating, to say the least...

If it doesn't start, or starts but then quits, one must turn the mags off, reprime, again pull the prop through until it is in one of the two good positions, put the switches back on, and try again. It's very labor intensive, and if one doesn't hit it just right one can be quite tired by the time one finally gets it running. Once when my second wife, Peggy (who was then my girlfriend, not yet having been promoted) and I took a Ryan to Mackinac Island, we stopped in Pellston on the way back for what we hoped was going to be a quick fuel stop, but I ended up propping the plane for two hours before it finally caught and ran. And all that was done with two broken ribs, the result of a water skiing incident several days before the trip. That two-hour delay put us far enough behind that we had to spend an unplanned overnight in Clare, Michigan, when it became obvious we would not make it back to Ann Arbor before dark. The rodeo was in town in Clare, and we got the last motel room available. Even with the rodeo beckoning, by that time my broken ribs were hurting so bad it was all I could do to fall into bed at the motel and try to recover enough to prop the Ryan again the next morning. Ah, the pleasures of flying antique airplanes.

The thrill of the limited aerobatics my father showed me in the Taylorcraft always stayed with me, and now I had a plane that could do anything I wanted. The Ryan came with two parachutes, but they were old surplus units, and even after I had them inspected and repacked they still fit funny. They were backpacks, and the Ryan was designed with bucket seats, so what I really needed were standard military seat pack parachutes. I traded the two backpacks to a local parachute loft for two new military seat pack chutes, and I was in business.

It's never a good idea to teach yourself something as critical as aerobatics, but being young and full of confidence and testosterone, I figured I was up to it. My father had cautioned me about the PT-22 and its nasty stall characteristics, and he suggested I should first strap on the chute and go up to three or four thousand feet and explore the slow flight and stall characteristics, both in coordinated and cross-controlled flight. Sounded like good advice, so I picked a nice summer day and did exactly that. Dad knew what he was talking about, and what I found was sobering.

The PT-22 had a very abrupt stall. With power at idle and the plane pointed straight ahead, the stall came with little warning, but other than that was relatively vice less. When the same maneuver was attempted with power on, or in a turn (especially a cross-controlled turn), though, the little open cockpit plane went sharply over the top into a spin before I could blink an eye. I was used to spins, as spin training and practice was a standard part of learning to fly in those days, so the recovery was effected without problem, but it took 1,000' of altitude before the plane was under full control again. I could see why my dad's advice was so valuable. The thousand-foot recovery cushion required was the reason so many pilots were killed in Ryans in stall/spin accidents in the airport traffic pattern. Standard pattern altitude was (and still is) 800', so stalling a Ryan turning from base to final, especially if you were not in coordinated flight, was a good way to become a statistic. From that day on, I never did aerobatics in my Ryan unless I was at least 3,000' above the ground.

I could see that, with those stall characteristics, the PT-22 was going to be a great snap roll airplane, so I asked another friend, Jim Mynning (who had owned a Ryan in the past), what speed I should use for entry. His answer was "the book says 105, but try 115 or 120 – it snaps much better." So up I went, and at 4,500' I pushed the nose over to 120mph, pulled up to plus 10 degrees pitch, and promptly jammed the stick back while pushing full left rudder. The plane hesitated just a second, and I could feel the shudder as it broke free and did a snap roll to the left. Wow! I figured that I should lead the pullout by 90 degrees of roll, as that's the same lead required for active spin recovery in a PT-22, so after 270 degrees of roll, I neutralized the controls. Presto! I was fully recovered and in level flight seemingly only a couple of seconds after snap entry! I was thrilled, and after half a dozen more, I decided to return to the hangar at Ann Arbor, where a refrigerator full of cold beer awaited me with which to celebrate.

Loops were difficult in the Ryan. It had such bad stall habits that I only tried a few of those. I always worried about stalling it out on the top of the loop, and ending up in an inverted spin. Those are all concerns that I voiced once to Bill Barber (remember Bill? He's the one who "arranged" the sale of my old Aeronca Champ). Bill offered to give me some instruction in aerobatics in the Ryan, and I eagerly took him up on it. We went up together one afternoon and Bill taught me several basic maneuvers. Communication was difficult, as the PT-22 had no intercom, but he briefed me well on the ground, and we agreed he'd throttle back so I could hear him as he shouted (!!) instructions to me between maneuvers. I learned a lot from Bill, and have fond memories of me doing a roll in the Ryan, at the conclusion of which Bill throttled back and yelled "that was good, but use a bit more rudder…"

Fun times.

Airplane #8: 1940 Ryan ST3-KR N50644

The summer of open cockpits, 1978, was wonderful. When I was not flying for North Central, I spent my days at Ann Arbor Airport. Everyone has a specific time in his/her life to which they fondly refer as their Golden Years, and the years 1977-1979 were that period for me. I was a young airline pilot with a wonderful girlfriend and an open cockpit airplane, with no obligations. It just doesn't get any better than that. I think often of those days...

I flew the Ryan often, and spent many hours keeping it looking good with metal polish and wax. On one of those days, I was waxing the wooden propeller on the PT-22, when a man walked up behind me and began chatting. I was used to that, as the Ryan was like a people magnet. This day, though, it was different. He said my plane looked good, and interestingly enough he knew where there was another one of these that had been abandoned in a barn. My ears perked up. I already had one Ryan, and should have been satisfied, but I knew I had to hear more. I slowly got the information from him about where this "mystery airplane" was located, and I proceeded to go there later in my car. His directions were good, although the "barn" was actually an old hangar on a private farm airstrip, and the plane wasn't "abandoned," but rather just in long-term storage (with WAY overdue hangar rent, so maybe it WAS abandoned after all). It sat under several years' worth of dust and bird droppings, surrounded by two spare engines and many boxes of miscellaneous spare parts. Treasure!

I rang the doorbell on the farmhouse, and was greeted by the lady of the house. I told her the story of how I knew about the abandoned Ryan on her property, and asked if she knew anything about it. She said she would consider it a great favor if I could arrange to remove it (after, of course, she had been paid for all the back hangar rent...). I told her I'd try, and she gave me the name and address of the registered owner. I contacted him (not easy, as this was before cell phones, and he lived alone in a trailer and was never home), only to find he didn't want to sell. I kept after him, though, and he weakened. The final thing that convinced him to sell was my promise that his PT-22 would be restored to flying status, not "parted out." He reluctantly agreed to sell, and I quickly paid him and filed the paperwork before he could change his mind.

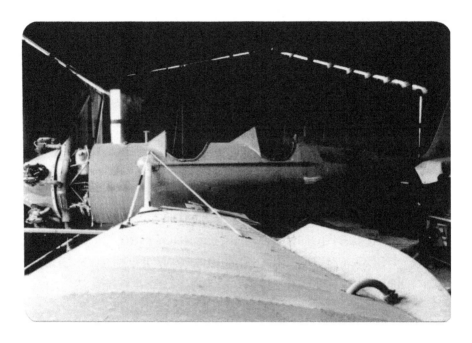

It's every antique airplane fanatic's dream to locate an abandoned plane covered with bird poop, and retrieve and restore it. I was about to live that dream. Once the plane was mine, I enlisted the help of good friends and fellow airline pilots Joe Vallee and Bruce Heiss in dismantling and moving it to my hangar at Ann Arbor. I will always remember the day Joe and I went to start the recovery process with a trailer. We removed the wings to put them on the trailer, but left the engine and prop on the fuselage, which was still on the landing gear.

By this time I had finished not just one but two degrees in Aerospace Engineering, so I had no excuse whatsoever for not predicting what came next. I did not take into account the dramatic shift forward in center of gravity of the fuselage/engine assembly without the fairly heavy wings attached, and the fuselage was very light on the tail in that configuration. So light, in fact, that when I lifted the tail to move it, the fuselage snapped itself from my hands and tipped up on its nose! After it started, I was powerless to do anything but watch it go. Luckily, by this time, we had moved it out of the hangar to have more room in which to work, so the tail simply ended up ten feet in the air, with the nose sitting unceremoniously in the mud. Had it happened in the hangar with a low ceiling, it would have been a completely different story.

The fact that it had been raining during the previous week left the sod very soft, so nothing was hurt but my pride. Joe and I had a good laugh after looking quickly around to make sure no one saw it but us! It became obvious that using a flatbed trailer wasn't going to work, so the actual transport of the fuselage assembly was done later using a hired flatbed truck with a winch to load the fuselage nose first. Needless to say, much care was given to prevent a recurrence of the tip-up!

Back home at Ann Arbor Airport, I put the new/old Ryan in the hangar with my airworthy one. It was a tight fit, with Ryan parts and engines everywhere, but I knew I wasn't going to be flying my assembled one for a few months, so it was fine for the winter. I'd have from November until spring to get a plan of action.

That plan presented itself one day in a chat with Mary Rosasco in the airport office, when she told me there was another tee hangar for rent very close to my present one. I told her I'd take it, and as soon as spring weather broke I moved all the Ryan parts to the new hangar. I now had all the pieces in place for a summer that was even more pleasant than the last one. I didn't think it could ever get better than the summer of 1978, but the summer of 1979 was about to surpass that!

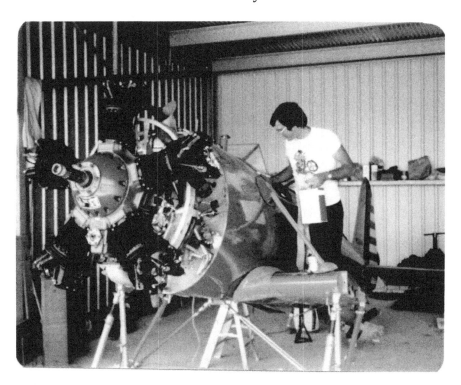

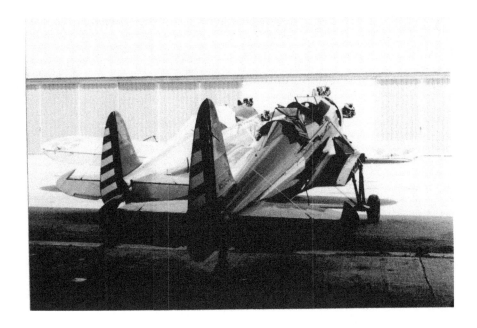

I now had one flying Ryan PT-22, and one more to work on. On the good days I flew the airworthy one through the warm summer skies of southern Lower Michigan, doing loops, snap rolls and spins, and returned to the hangar to put the plane away and have a beer from the hangar fridge. On the days when the weather wasn't so good, I had the other plane a short walk away in the other hangar. I steadily made progress on that project, first cleaning up the years of accumulated dirt on the various items, then cataloguing the boxes of parts, then fixing and reassembling the structure. I did all this under the guidance of Gary Cady, a very capable mechanic who had helped me with my other planes over the years. Eventually, the second hangar ended up going from a hangar full of Ryan parts & pieces to a hangar with a second flyable airplane, surrounded by piles of spares. It was time for a test flight.

After working on the plane for months, I donned a helmet and my dad swung the prop. The Kinner R-56 came to life, and I taxied out. After a short distance, I detected a fault in the tail wheel, so came to a stop and shut the engine down. It was an easy fix, so I restarted and continued taxiing to the runway. All senses on the alert for more problems, I advanced the throttle for takeoff and soon the Ryan I rescued from a dusty storage once again took to the air! I was elated. After I landed and taxied in, my father wanted a turn, so we swapped places and I swung the prop for him. He took off and after about 30 minutes, he arrived back at the hangar. He got out with a smile on his face, and pronounced the airplane fit for use. Concerned for my safety, he said he had put the PT-22 through its paces, pulling enough plus and minus g's to test the plane's structural integrity. His smile told me everything – I had not one but two solid, flyable PT-22s!

Ryan PT-22s had their dark side, as described above. The abrupt stall characteristics killed more than a few PT-22 owners in airport traffic patterns, so when it came time to move it along, rather than sell it, I thought it would be a better idea to donate it to a museum. The Airpower Museum in Blakesburg, Iowa said they'd be delighted to have it, so that's where it went. I believe it's still part of their collection today.

Airplane #9 - Cessna 140 N77174

Peggy and I, now married, moved to Minneapolis in the summer of 1980. I had been "promoted" to Director of Flight Standards for Republic Airlines. I say promoted, but it sure didn't feel like a promotion. It was a management office job that allowed me to keep my number on the line pilots' seniority list. I got an office with a window, which was both a blessing and a curse. The blessing: I got to watch the airliners take off and land from the comfort of my office. The curse: I was forced to watch the airliners take off and land from the comfort of my office... WITHOUT ME. I was born to fly, and had the greatest job in the world, that of an airline pilot. I never went to work, I just went flying. In the office, however, I was chained to a telephone and an inbox/outbox on my desk. It took me only a short time to realize that I was not really happy outside of a cockpit. My salvation was the very occasional line trip for which I tore myself away from the desk, and the weekend flying I did with my Ryan.

Summer turned to fall. That meant winter was coming, though, and this was Minnesota. As the saying goes, "there's nothing between Minnesota and the North Pole but a barbed wire fence." The open cockpit Ryan was not going to cut it for the long, cold winter. I began to search for a four-season airplane to replace the Ryan.

The Cessna 120/140 series held many great memories for me, and was at the top of my list of year round planes. In October 1980, I found a possible one for sale in Novato, California. It was a beautiful example of a rag wing Cessna 140. Best of all, the owners, two brothers named Rick and Gary Thompson, were searching for an open cockpit plane like the Ryan to enjoy in the California sun. With the possibility of a trade in the offing, I went to California to see the 140.

N77174 was a beauty. Restored very nicely with a custom paint job, it would look great in my hangar in Minnesota. We struck a deal in short order. We would swap airplanes with a stack of cash also changing hands. Ownership would transfer with the airplanes sitting where they were, meaning I would pick up the 140 in California and fly it back to Minnesota, and Rick and/or Gary would retrieve the Ryan and fly it to California. Considering the approaching winter, I probably got the better of that part of the deal.

I was excited about the upcoming trip across the country, and told many of my coworkers in the office back at the airline about it. One friend in particular, Mark Thelen, an aeronautical engineer in Republic Airlines' performance engineering department, wanted to hear more. He was a private pilot who had never flown a tail dragger, and said he'd love to get some time in a 140. I asked if he'd be interested in an adventure, accompanying me on the trek across the desert and through the Rockies with my new purchase, and he jumped at the chance. So, we watched the weather, packed a couple of duffel bags, and in late October off we went to California.

Mark was as big a guy as I was (6' and probably 180-200#), so with our overnight gear and some tools we were maxed out for every takeoff. The 140 had a nice strong engine, though, and we picked airports with long paved runways, so the trip was uneventful from a performance point of view. In addition, the weather was perfect. For several days, we saw nothing but blue skies. On the last day, we saw the first cloud cover, which was a high layer of cirrus. Mark got a tail wheel checkout on the way, and the airplane was put in the hangar at Flying Cloud Airport in Minneapolis. The first ride I gave, of course, was Peggy, who pronounced it a fine addition to the family.

The lure of line flying was too strong for me. After a year of watching airliners land from my office window, I decided to pick up my flight kit and return to the line. Not to disparage the office environment, but for a pilot whose heart was in the cockpit, it was like crawling out from under a rock. I returned to the Detroit base, and Peg and I moved back to our beloved Ann Arbor, taking N77174 back to my old hangar at Ann Arbor Airport. I must have seen it coming, as I had simply sublet the hangar to one of my airline friends when I left for the office, so all I had to do was give him a call and I had the hangar back.

Airplane #10 - 1941 Piper J-3 N38822

The 140 was great fun, but there was one airplane type I'd never owned, and knew that eventually I must: the Piper J-3 Cub. The J-3 was so iconic in aviation history that for decades all light airplanes were referred to generically as "Piper Cubs" regardless of their actual type. The Cub taught generations to fly, went to war with the USAAF in WWII, and later was the "everyman's airplane." It remains legendary to this day.

In June 1982, I moved N77174 along to an eager buyer who wanted a good Cessna 140, and he got one when he bought mine. I began my search for a Cub. It took a year, but in June of 1983 I found one fairly nearby, right up the road in Lansing, Michigan.

The price was low, so I cautiously went to take a look. What I found was a J-3 that had definitely seen better days. The fabric was old, and one of the wings looked as if it had mouse damage to the rib stitches under the fabric. It flew well, though, and I went to a local coffee shop with the seller to talk about it. I mentioned the "average" condition of the plane, and emphasized the mouse damage in the wing, and shot him a ridiculously low offer. He didn't miss a beat, and looked across the table at me and said "Okay, sold." Omigosh, I was about to own a real live honest to goodness Piper J-3 Cub.

I paid the man and returned to pick the plane up. I fired it up, flew it to Ann Arbor, and put it in the hangar. My father came to inspect my new purchase, and took one look at the damaged rib stitching in the left wing, and promptly pronounced the plane unairworthy. In retrospect, I really don't know what I was thinking when I flew the plane home like that, but I suppose it's a testament to the Cub that it could fly with bad stitching. No wonder the seller jumped at my offer – I probably could have offered him half of that, and he'd still have jumped at it.

I grounded the plane while I figured out my next move. As a quick fix, my father suggested that we simply leave the still-serviceable fabric on the wing and just re-stitch and re-tape it. That sounded good to me, so that's what we did. The plane was soon back in the air, and I have many wonderful memories of flying that J-3 in southern lower Michigan the next summer. I owned that Cub until the summer of 1986, having finally decided to recover the wings and tail along the way. The entire plane was painted, too, so when I sold it, it looked like a brand new nickel.

John F. Hanson

Airplane #11 - 1946 Piper J-3 N24946

The Cub experience must have been stronger than I expected, because I instantly regretted disposing of my J-3. Two years passed, during which I never tired of saying how much I wanted my Cub back to whoever was listening. Peggy got fed up with my moping about it, and said if I missed it that much, I should just go buy another one. Why didn't I think of that? Excellent suggestion.

As it happened, I soon flew a Republic Airlines line trip with a copilot named Gary Burch. I told him the whole tale, and mentioned I was shopping for another J-3. He said, "Why don't you just buy mine? I've got one for sale." I did a double take at the serendipity! As soon as we finished flying the trip, we met at Napoleon, Michigan, where the plane was hangared. It was a beautiful little blue and white Cub, and had the upgraded 85hp Continental engine with a metal prop. Recently restored, it was much nicer than the one I sold two years before. We soon struck a deal, and in August 1988 I once again had a Piper Cub in my hangar at Ann Arbor. I based that Cub at Ann Arbor until June of 1989.

Many things were happening in the airline industry at that time. Republic Airlines had become part of Northwest Airlines, and my history in flight ops management at Republic came back to haunt me. I was offered a position as the Boeing 727 Manager in Flight Standards at Northwest. The frustrating experience in the office at Republic was a distant memory, and being a slow learner, I accepted the desk at Northwest. I knew that if it didn't work out I could always go back to the line, since I would keep the all important seniority number.

So it came to be that in June 1989, I flew my beloved J-3 from Ann Arbor to Minneapolis, where it was to live in a succession of hangars. Starting at a hangar at Crystal Airport, then Flying Cloud Airport, I eventually found a t-hangar at Faribault, Minnesota. I owned that Cub for seven years, the longest I had ever owned any single airplane.

Airplane #12 – 1941 Piper J-4

While I owned the J-3, I found myself in the habit of enjoying Saturday morning coffee and sweet rolls with friends at Roy Redman's hangar at Faribault airport. It was always a fine time of eating donuts and telling caffeine-fueled lies, and one Saturday morning someone said he knew of a Piper J-4 for sale on a trailer, with a freshly overhauled engine. The airframe was in need of total restoration, and was unbelievably cheap. Hmmm, this might be fun, I thought – a J-3 to fly, and a J-4 to work on! He had the guy's phone number, so I called him from right there at the hangar. Yes, he had the plane, and it was dismantled "but all the pieces were there." Yes, it was all loaded on the trailer, and for the low price he'd also throw in the trailer. It was all located about a fifteen minute drive from my parents' house. As it happened, my father was driving his van up the next day for a visit, and could just swing by the fellow's hangar and hook up the trailer. It all came together too easily, so I told the seller I'd take it. My dad could pay him when he hooked up the trailer, and I'd reimburse him when he got to Minneapolis. Two days later, the J-4 was sitting in my hangar next to the J-3.

I was about to learn some difficult and expensive lessons. First, the plane that was supposedly "all there" wasn't all there. Some very important and strategic (and expensive, hard to find…) parts were missing. But worse, when I went to register the purchase with the FAA Aircraft Registry, I found that the seller didn't technically own the plane to start with! I called him and asked why he hadn't registered the sale when he bought it, and his answer was very vague. I decided to call the fellow he had purchased the plane from, to see if he could help me set the chain of ownership right with the FAA. When I told him what was going on, he was understandably furious. He began yelling on the phone, saying he had already signed one bill of sale, and wasn't going to sign another. I was going to be the one stuck holding the bag unless I could get him to settle down. To make a long story short, I made the point that I was a victim as much as he was, and he finally did help me get the papers right so I owned the plane. It couldn't fix the problem, however, of the missing rare parts, so in frustration I decided to take a loss and sell the plane, just to get it out of my hangar and my life. I was very happy to see it go.

I learned two lessons the hard way with that plane. First, never buy a plane, especially a "project plane," unless you personally inspect it and fly it. Of course, that lesson should have already been learned with the Cessna 120 experience (see Airplane #5 chapter), but as I said, I'm a slow learner. If it's in pieces, make absolutely sure it's all there before giving the seller any money. Second, always do a title search on any plane before you buy it to be certain the seller really owns it. Had I done either of those two things with the J-4, it never would have left Illinois for Minnesota on the trailer. Come to think of it, the trailer was actually the most trouble free part of that purchase.

Airplane #13: 1973 Cessna 180 N9798G

The Piper Cub phase of my life had been wonderful. Owning a J-3 is something every pilot should do at least once. But it all came to an end in December 1995, when my father was giving my nephew Jimmy a ride in the J-3 and the engine quit at about 200' on takeoff. Dad did exactly what he should, landing it straight ahead, but he ran out of airport before he ran out of speed, and flipped the poor Cub on its back. No one was hurt, thank God, but the Cub was bent up pretty bad. So bad, in fact, that the insurance company elected to "total" the plane, and wrote me a check for the full insured amount.

I had never carried in-motion hull insurance on any of my planes, thinking, "I'm a big boy, if I break it I'll fix it…" But about a year before the incident, as I was chatting with the insurance agent on the phone when I renewed my policy on the J-3, he said, "I see you don't have the aircraft hull insured while in motion. You are basically saying that if you wreck the plane, you have so much money that it truly won't phase you to buy the same plane twice." I thought about that for a minute, asked how much the hull in-motion insurance premium was, and then for the first time in my life I bought the coverage. Just about a year later, I stood looking at my totaled Cub, but could take some small comfort in knowing it was now the insurance company's airplane. They paid me with no questions asked. I said a prayer of thanks that no one was hurt, and began thinking about my next plane.

Having obtained my commercial, instrument, and flight instructor ratings in dad's 1961 Cessna 180 when I was a teenager, I had always had a soft spot in my heart for the 180, and put that type at the top of my shopping list. As luck would have it, I found a 1973 180J for sale at Lake Elmo airport in Minnesota, quite close to where I lived in Northfield. I went up and took a look, flew it, liked what I saw, and shot him an offer. He took it, so (after a professional pre-buy inspection AND title search this time!) in the summer of 1996 I was on my way to having a Cessna 180 in my life again.

This plane came with floats and hydraulic wheel skis, which were both something new to me. I had no use for either one, since I don't live on a lake, and my home airport of Faribault keeps the pavement quite clean, so skis were not required equipment. Trailering the floats home was a project in itself, as straight floats are wiiiiide when assembled (as these were), and would not fit comfortably on the trailer I used. I had to build a rack for them and they still were probably wider than was legal, so I stuck to the back rural roads. Probably lucky I wasn't stopped...

Flying a 180 again after so many years was a thrill. The first time I taxied out alone after the purchase was complete, it was like being a teenager again. I had forgotten how much fun a 180 was! It was (and still is) pretty nearly a perfect airplane. Bush pilots hold the Cessna 180 and 185 models in very high regard, for good reason. They can haul a big load, legendary in fact. They can operate out of unimproved airstrips, taking off and landing from hillsides, riverbeds, gravel roads, etc. They cruise at very decent speeds, and are also great float and ski airplanes. Having my own 180 was a wonderful experience. I could play bush pilot all the time – well, at least in my own head. I was in pilot heaven, flying airliners for a living and having a Cessna 180 as a toy. The whole family had fun with this one, as the four seats allowed me to host hangar barbecues for my daughters' friends, which included rides for everybody!

Airplane #14 - 1943 Boeing A75N1 Stearman N60961

They say that the course of your life can be affected by the smallest of events. A passing image can catch you in just the right mood, and leave its mark in your brain, affecting you for the rest of your life. Musicians narrow their eyes and smile as they recount the first time they ever heard a piano or saw a cello, and say that they knew right then that they would play music for a living. When I was a young boy, probably about six or seven years old, one of those events happened to me (but not with a piano or cello…). It was an overcast day, and I was riding in the right seat of a car driven by one of my parents. I was just watching the world go by out the window, when a yellow biplane going the same direction passed us. Since his speed was only slightly faster than our speed, I had lots of time to look at this beautiful plane. It was a Boeing Model 75, commonly known as a Stearman. The magic of that yellow Navy paint job, the radial engine, and the open cockpits impressed me so much I was speechless. Even at that young age, I knew instantly that some day I'd have one of those!

I never forgot that afternoon in the car, and carried the images and feeling of sighting that first Stearman with me for the rest of my life. Every time I opened Trade-A-Plane, the Stearman listings always got at least a cursory scan, and I'd think "Hmmm, some day, some day…" The Stearmans at air shows and breakfast flights never failed to get a visit from me, and there was always a smile on my face as I walked around one.

I came close to buying one a couple times over the years. I put a deposit on one in Harvard, Illinois, once, but certification and paperwork issues changed my mind on that one. My parents had relocated to Spruce Creek Fly-in in Daytona Beach, Florida, which can best be described as Pilot Heaven. Basically an airport and golf resort with an elaborate and well-planned layout of taxiways and lots, with a large runway right down the middle, most homes had their own hangar adjacent to the house. Golf carts were the order of the day even if you didn't golf, since you could drive around on the taxiways and spend your days in the warm Florida sun stopping at friends' hangars and talking airplanes. In that environment, Stearmans seemed to be everywhere.

My father had a succession of planes at Daytona Beach. Anyone who has ever said to me "Wow, you sure do trade planes often" got this response from me: "That's nothing compared to the list of airplanes my dad's had." My father was retired from the airline, and not only had planes of his own, but flew them for others as well. He was a ferry pilot for the popular air show act the "Eagles Aerobatic Team," and also flew Gene Soucy's Extra from show to show.

Dad was also flying the DC-3 for the Valiant Air Command, an organization that was devoted to maintaining and flying aircraft from World War II. My father had somewhere just short of 20,000 hours of DC-3 time dating from his years as a pilot for North Central Airlines, and had been a check pilot on that type of airplane for years, so he was a natural to help out with the VAC in taking their Dakota to and from air shows, and flying it in the shows as well. I recall vividly once going with him to one of those shows, and flying along when he dropped the Army Golden Knights parachute team at the show. The door had been removed from the plane, leaving a large cargo sized opening at the back of the cabin. As dad climbed the DC-3 to the jump altitude for the show, the team sat around on the floor casually chatting, wearing their chutes. We made a few passes through the jump zone as the jump master judged the wind by watching a streamer they had dropped, then decided the next run would be the "hot" run. He gave the sign that it was almost time to go, and the team rose to their feet. We reached the jump point, and when he gave the "go" signal, I'll never forget the sight of about twenty men running at full speed and leaping out that big door of the DC-3 as close together as they could get. One minute the plane was full of jumpers wearing their gear, and seemingly a few seconds later the cabin was empty, with only the wind blowing through. It was a very strange and wonderful experience.

The Valiant Air Command also had a hangar that served as their museum, and between shows they had many planes on display. In the time he flew for the VAC, he spent much time over there. One day he called me in Minnesota, and told me of a Stearman that had been on display there for quite some time. The owner had let them keep it there indefinitely since he had moved from Florida, and Dad had heard that the owner was now thinking of just selling it. He asked if I wanted him to call the fellow and make an offer, since he knew I'd always wanted a Stearman. I asked a few questions about the plane, and it became obvious that it had not even been run in quite some time. There were lots of question marks, so I told him that I didn't want to offer more than "project price," as we didn't know what we were going to find if and when we rolled it out and tried to run it. We might find a plane that was actually flyable, or we might find that it needed a total rebuild. We settled on offering an amount that would leave me some room to fix a significant number of things that might be bad after such a long time of inactivity in the Florida salt air. Dad said he'd call the guy and see what happened.

I didn't dare get my hopes up, since I'd wanted one for so long, and told myself that even if I got this one, there'd be some issues (possibly very expensive ones) in putting it back in service after such a long period of inactivity. I went about my business, and one day about a week later I was in my hangar playing with the Cessna 180, when my cell phone rang. It was Dad, who said, "Hello, is this the newest Stearman owner in Minnesota?" I smiled broadly, as he told me the fellow had taken the offer. So, many years after seeing the yellow Stearman in Wisconsin that had lit the flame in me, I had finally made the connection. I closed the deal in April 1998, and I had my Stearman!

We would soon find out if my fears about problems from long-term storage were justified. My father was in Florida, and I was in Minnesota, so it just made sense to have him just go over and see if the plane ran (or not) as a first step. He agreed to go over and roll the plane out and hit the starter. He said he'd do just that and call me back. The next day he phoned, and was optimistic. He said he went over to the VAC, rolled the ship out, and for the first time saw it in the daylight. He checked out all the systems to see if everything seemed functional, and decided to just charge the battery and swing the prop to see what happened. He said it started without delay, and seemed to run normally! We agreed that the next step would be to fly the plane the short distance to Spruce Creek, so that we could investigate further in the comfort and privacy of Dad's hangar. As he did that, I would catch the next flight to Daytona Beach, so we could knock off the rough edges and finish preparing the Stearman for the trip to its new home up north.

As soon as my Northwest Airlines duties allowed, I caught a plane to Florida. Arriving at Spruce Creek, I got my first look at the plane I had waited a half-century to own and then bought sight unseen. I was certainly not disappointed. It was an older restoration, but seemed to be in "serviceable" condition. I was happy with my decision to make my offer low enough to account for possible problems, though, as we still had to find out if the engine was going to need any work.

My father said that it had vibrated quite noticeably on the short ferry flight to Spruce Creek, although it ran well in all other respects. The plane was equipped with a ground adjustable McCauley propeller, which was the most likely source of the vibration. I was anxious to fly the plane, but we decided we'd first correct the prop problem. We started it up in front of dad's hangar, and just the sound of that Continental 220 radial barking at idle set my pulse racing. However, I ran it up to 1500 RPM, and the vibration was painfully obvious.

"Ground adjustable" props are exactly that, propellers on which a mechanic can manually set the prop blade angles independently, and if the blades are not set at precisely the same angle, a vibration can result. The greater the difference between the two angles, the worse the vibration. We grabbed a prop protractor and set to work. We adjusted the angles, ran it again to check for vibration, shut it down, adjusted again, and so forth, until after a couple of hours we deemed it cured. The final step was a test flight, for which I could hardly wait. We strapped in and swung the prop. I taxied out, checked for traffic, and took off. I'll never forget that flight. The plane flew well, and the sound of that radial, coupled with the wind in my face, told me that I had some very pleasant flying time waiting for me.

I had to return home to do some more flying for Northwest, but we agreed that it would be a fun adventure for us both if we flew it from Florida to Minnesota together. I would go home to work, but would return as soon as practical to fly it to Minnesota with dad.

When I was free, however, the weather was lousy for open cockpit cross-countries, so we waited. After two weeks of several such disappointing cycles, we decided that when the weather finally looked favorable, dad would simply start north with the Stearman, even if I weren't there to start the trip with him. Then, if it came to that, I'd join up with him as soon as I could en route.

That's exactly what happened. The weather broke, and I was still a day away from being able to go join him, so he started the trip without me, heading for Memphis. I was free the next day, so I took the airline to Memphis and joined him there. When we left Memphis northbound in my Stearman, I thought I was in heaven. We flew several legs from Memphis to my hangar in Faribault, Minnesota, with no further weather problems, and on May 5, 1998, the plane was at last in my hangar. It ran well en route, and the propeller problems were obviously solved.

Posing with my Stearman, at last.

These two are pictures of my daughter Christine, wearing a parachute that probably weighed about half what she did!

The plane now shared a hangar with my Cessna 180, and it was quite crowded in there. So crowded, in fact that I began to talk with Peg about how we should perhaps sell the 180. She was very emphatic about how she thought that would be a mistake. She said that I'd seemed so happy with the 180 that I'd be nuts to sell it. She said her opinion was that each plane served its own purpose, and if I sold the 180 I'd regret it. I said, "Duly noted," and then promptly sold the 180. Good 180s (and mine was good...) sell quickly, which mine did.

For the record, Peggy was right. Not a month goes by that I don't wish I had that 180 back. Lessons learned: first, when you get a plane you love, and don't have to sell it, DON'T; and second, listen to your wife.

After a wonderful, magical summer of flying, I decided that it was time for that old radial engine to get a close inspection. Since it had been many years since it was last overhauled, I removed the engine and sent it off to the good folks at Radial Engines Ltd in Guthrie, Oklahoma for a complete major overhaul. It came back shining better than new, with everything good inside, and I put it back on the Stearman. I also had decided to put on a new wood prop instead of the metal McCauley, and it gave the plane a wonderful vintage look.

I flew that plane until April 2002, when I delivered it to its new owner. I had decided to sell it because it had been quite some time since its last restoration, and I knew if I kept it more than a few more years, I would face the decision of how best to restore it. I decided to pass it along to someone while it still had several good years left on the last restoration, so the new owner could have some fun with it before he restored it. I explained it that way to an eager looker, who said that approach was fine with him.

Over the previous four years, I had fulfilled my childhood dream, living my own version of what I felt when that yellow Stearman had passed our car a half century before. Along the way, I gave over eighty people their first open cockpit airplane ride. I had owned many airplanes, but the Stearman was hands down the most magical of them all.

Airplane #15 -1946 Cessna 140 N2724N

My hangar at Faribault Airport was built on land leased from the city, and on that lease was a provision that the hangar was primarily for storage of an airplane. This was to avoid the situation wherein someone might build a hangar and proceed to use it only to store refrigerators or tractors or cars or widgets. I had no problems with that provision, but there was an ominous clause in the lease that said that if you got rid of your plane, you had only ninety days in which to buy another. When I sold the Stearman, the 90-day clock started ticking, so I was again shopping.

I started looking for something "interesting," and what I found was another Cessna 140. The plane was actually found by my brother, since it was being used for rental and tail wheel instruction at Poplar Grove Airport, his home base in Illinois. He said it had just been advertised for sale, so I went down and took a look. Slipping into that 140 brought back lots of memories. It was like putting on a comfortable old bedroom slipper, and to make a long story short, in May 2002, I bought it. Having another 140 was like being able to spend time with an old friend. I went to breakfast fly-ins, gave rides, and generally had a ball.

Cessna 120s and 140s, siblings that were distinguishable early in their lives by the presence of flaps, a rear window, and an electrical system on the more deluxe 140, were billed as suitable transportation airplanes in the late 1940s. The ads had a "businessman" (never a "businesswoman," a sign of the times...) with a briefcase flying to their next appointment with a 140. The plane was an efficient way to get from A to B back then, and with very few modifications it's still true. Thus it was that on one fine summer's day I decided to take the 140 to a reunion of retired North Central Airlines pilots and their families at the small airport in New Richmond, Wisconsin. I had offered to bring the sweet corn, so I packed the 140 right seat and baggage compartment with bag after bag of delicious corn supplied by Dave Hagen, a dear family friend who raised and sold what was quite possibly the world's sweetest and best sweet corn. My folks were already there with their motor home, and I took off with the 140 in plenty of time to get there for a nice visit before the festivities started.

It was a great day for flying, and I took off at Faribault and set a course northeast for New Richmond. I'd be there in less than an hour, compared to the about-two hours it would have taken had I driven. I was enjoying the smooth morning air, smug about how easy and fun this would be, when the airplane shuddered violently and began to vibrate so intensely I couldn't even read the instruments. I was still climbing, and only ten miles or so northeast of Faribault, so I instinctively began a turn to return, while applying carburetor heat and reducing power to try to remedy the vibration. Nothing helped, although reducing the power seemed to lessen the vibration somewhat. Although I was still flying and the plane was shaking badly, the power the engine was producing was a fraction of what it should have been, and it was obvious I might not make it back to the airport.

Faribault had a grass runway that was very nearly aligned with my heading as I returned. Since the engine was running (sort of), my plan was to leave the power at its current setting. I feared that if I messed with the throttle any more it would probably just quit. I kept one eye on the grass runway ahead, and continually scanned for other traffic and suitable fields into which I could glide if worse came to worst. There were gliders being launched with a tow plane all day at Faribault, and if I encountered one of those I'd really have some maneuvering to do, as they are limited in the evasive action they can take. It looked like it was going to be a flip of the coin as to whether I'd make the field. That was the longest ten miles I'd ever flown, but through very judicious handling of pitch and a prayer to whoever in heaven was in charge of poor aviators that day, I just barely arrived over the end of the grass runway at a height of about twenty feet.

I knew I had the field made at that point, so pulled the throttle to idle and the propeller instantly stopped cold. I flared and touched down in blessed silence. I must have been quite a sight, as I'm sure I was out of the plane before it stopped rolling. I was afraid of fire, and didn't intend to be in my cute little 140 if it was about to burst into flames. Had that happened, I'd have ended up with about seven large bags of sweet corn, roasted in a very unorthodox manner.

I was still looking for signs of smoke or fluid leakage when J.C. Cunningham, a good friend who ran the glider operation, drove up with the car he used to tow the gliders to their launch point. He asked if I was OK. I eyed the fifty feet of rope attached to his trailer hitch, and thought for a moment before replying, "J.C., there's only one thing better than having a good friend ask if I'm OK after an experience like that, and that's having the friend ask it from behind the wheel of a car that has a fifty foot tow rope attached!"

He looked at the plane, which was now sitting quietly, and said, "hook 'er up, let's get it back to your hangar." Sounded good to me. We towed the 140 and all that corn back and rolled the plane into the hangar. I thanked J.C, and he took off to run the busy glider operation. I opened the cowling on the plane, and stood looking for signs of the distress that almost put me into a farmer's field somewhere only twenty minutes before. There were no signs at all of anything wrong. I knew that couldn't be the case, though, so I assumed the failure had been inside the engine somewhere. At any rate, the plane was obviously not in any danger of exploding or burning at that point, so I decided it might be time to look at what I could salvage of the rest of the day.

I was still expected at the reunion picnic in New Richmond, and I had all the corn still in the plane. I looked at my watch and was glad I had decided to take off early for the party, since I now still had time to make the drive in my pickup and arrive with the corn for everybody to enjoy. I quickly swapped the load to the pickup box, gave the plane a kiss and a promise, closed the hangar door, and left.

The friends at the picnic were happy to see me, although I suspect the seven bags of sweet corn were what they welcomed most. My folks were a little surprised to see me show up with a truck instead of an airplane. When I told my father what had happened, and that there were no visible signs of damage afterward, he thought for a second and suggested what I had already decided to do as soon as I got back to the hangar a few days later: pull the top spark plugs and check the compression on all four cylinders.

I returned to the hangar the next day, and didn't even have to get my compression tester out to find the culprit. Before I did anything, I simply pulled the prop through a few times, and immediately found that one cylinder had no compression at all. Zip. Zilch. Nada. I pulled the spark plugs, and again easily found the bad one. The right forward plug looked destroyed when I pulled it out. The electrode was gone, just pulverized. I got a flashlight and looked inside the cylinder, and saw a random collection of pieces of parts, and the top of the piston looked cratered like the surface of the moon. I knew that a valve must have come apart, and as it turned out that was exactly what had happened.

I called Wayne Trom, the mechanic who was helping me with the maintenance on the 140, and he came to the hangar with a spare cylinder and piston, and we pulled the bad one, keeping our fingers crossed that the damage had not gotten to the lower end. The cylinder and piston that we removed looked awful, but luckily the damage was confined to the upper end, and we fixed it with the parts Wayne supplied. The summer of flying continued!

But as much as I loved the 140, I knew something was missing. I missed the Stearman. Peggy could see it in my face when I came home from the hangar. She said I didn't come back with that sparkle in my eyes. She was right, and I could feel it too. The 140, as nice as it was, had been hurriedly purchased to fill my hangar, so I could comply with my hangar land lease requirement. Peggy encouraged me to just go find another Stearman, and that sounded like music to my ears.

I opened Trade-A-Plane and once again began searching. Not wanting to put myself in the position of selling before buying a replacement, though, this time I kept the 140 as I looked at Stearmans.

Airplane #16 - 1942 Boeing A75N1 Stearman N505V

The area south of Salinas, California, is sometimes known as "Steinbeck Country." It is a beautiful flat coastal valley, bordered by hills, extending south from Monterey Bay. Because of the climate and rich soil, it has been one of the best producers of vegetable crops in the nation. The flat terrain, coupled with the types of produce farmed there, made it an attractive and lucrative region for crop dusters after World War II.

The ready availability of the surplus Stearmans and copious stacks of spares available at bargain prices at war's end set the stage for the rugged biplane to become one of the most iconic crop dusters and sprayers in history. Of course, many of the planes ended up in Steinbeck Country, along with their mountains of spare parts.

I found a Stearman for sale in King City, in the heart of the area, and it looked like it was worth a trip out to California for an in-person inspection. Of course, considering the location, I suspected it was probably a former duster or sprayer, but decided to make the trip and see what kind of restoration it had undergone. I booked a cockpit jump seat on a Northwest A-320 to San Jose, and rented a car.

As I drove highway 101 from the San Jose Airport to King City, I called Peggy on the cell phone. It was a beautiful day for a drive, but my mind was elsewhere. I told her I was having second thoughts about spending "all that money on another Stearman, when I'd already had that experience." She pointed out that my mood had just not been the same since I sold my last one, and considering how short life is, we've all got to do what we can to fulfill our dreams, whenever possible. I again mentioned the cost, and she said, "No, you are going to drive down there, look at and fly that Stearman, and if it's a good one, you're going to buy it. Period."

What a gal. Have I mentioned how lucky I was to find her?

The Stearman, N505V, was being offered for sale by a retired duster/sprayer pilot named Gordon Plaskett. I went directly to his house, where I also met his wife, and they invited me to spend the night as their guest after I saw the plane. Without further delay, Gordon and I went to the King City Airport to see the Stearman.

My first Stearman had been finished with a civilian paint job, orange and white with wheel pants, pin striping, and a sunburst on the top wing. That had not been my first choice (remember I had bought that one sight unseen!), as I had always wanted one with a military paint scheme. One of the things that caught my eye about N505V was the USAAF paint job – blue fuselage, yellow wings and tail, striped rudder. It had what is referred to as the "Stars and Bars" paint. That was a definite plus.

I opened the plane up by removing as many of the panels as I could, which is quite easy to do on a Stearman (they were designed for easy maintenance in the field by 18-year old kids during WWII). What I found was very encouraging. The plane was in pristine condition inside and out. Gordon told me that this was the second time he had owned this plane, as it was first restored when a group of pilots in England contacted him about building up a fresh Stearman to ship to the U.K. for them. He did so, and the freshly restored Stearman went to England, where it was their pampered pet for over a decade. When they finally decided to sell it, they contacted Gordon and asked if he'd sell it for them in the U.S. He agreed, so the plane was sold back to Gordon, dismantled and shipped back to California, where Gordon and his mechanic reassembled it and reregistered in the U.S. as N505V. I asked him why he chose that particular number, and he said simply, "I've always liked fives." Whatever...

We rolled it out and went for a ride. It started right up, and I did the flying. I taxied it out, took off, and climbed to about 2,000', doing gradual turns. I leveled off and did some slow flight and a stall, and I was very impressed with the rigging on the Stearman – it flew hands off in cruise, something that would make for a much nicer trip if one were to fly the ship from California to, say, Minnesota...

On the way back to Gordon's house in his car, I said I liked the plane, and asked him if he was open to offers. I'm sure he could see the flecks of foam in the corners of my mouth and said, "Sorry, no." Shrewd seller.

I nodded my head and said, "OK, I'll take it." I drive a hard bargain.

I was on my way to owning another Stearman.

I made two phone calls from Gordon's house. The first was to Peggy, who was excited as I was. The second was to my father.

"Hey, Dad, Guess what I just bought!"

"What?

"Another Stearman! It's in California. You up for an adventure?"

"Sure! When do you want to go?"

And so yet another trip across the USA in an open cockpit biplane began to take shape. I returned home, and started to arrange the details. I ordered current Sectional charts (a LOT of them...), got my traveling tool kit ready, and dug out my old parachutes. The plane ran fine, but it still had yet to prove itself as reliable, and we had a lot of barren country to traverse, so we decided to wear the chutes "just in case." I packed it all up in two large boxes and sent them to Gordon's house FedEx, so they'd be there when we arrived.

I arranged for the funds, procured a blank Bill of Sale, and called the insurance company. All was set. Dad and I picked a week that looked as good as any, and we met in California.

The boxes were waiting for us. They were bigger than I recalled. I looked at them, then looked at the bags we had brought on the airline, then turned to my dad. He was thinking the same thing, and said,

"How are we going to fit all that stuff in a Stearman, along with two well fed pilots?"

I tried to be positive, and replied, "It'll work. Most of the contents of the boxes are the chutes."

We headed for the airport, anxious to get started. We rolled the Stearman out, did a preflight inspection, and started to transfer stuff from the rental car to the plane. The plan was for me to take off with the biplane and head for Bakersfield. At the same time, after I was safely airborne, dad would start for Bakersfield with the rental car, since we could not return it in King City.

I was tired, but it felt good to be in the air at last with my new Stearman. I managed to keep the Sectional chart from blowing out of the cockpit, and eventually Bakersfield crept into view. Our plan, formulated after so many cross country flights in both our pasts, was to make our stops at airports served by at least commuter airlines, in case the trip was interrupted by extended weather delays, or mechanicals on the as yet unproven airplane. I landed at Bakersfield, and taxied to the transient tie down area. I shut down, tied the plane down, and breathed a sigh of relief. It had been a long, long day.

I waited in the terminal for dad, who eventually showed up. A Stearman, which at 85 mph is NOT fast, is still faster than a car, if there's not a headwind. We were both ready to head for the hotel and a cold beer.

A good dinner and 8 hours sleep later, we arose and headed for breakfast, ready to continue the adventure. The plan was to head through the Tehachapi Pass just east of Bakersfield, and cross the Mojave Desert south of the huge airport that has been the stage for so much test flying in the jet age (read "The Right Stuff" for more details!), and also served as the landing area for the Space Shuttle. From there we would head for Barstow, CA, and then Kingman, AZ. Further stops would take us to Winslow, AZ, Albuquerque, NM, Amarillo, TX, Garden City, KS, Salina, KS, Omaha, NB, Fort Dodge, IA, and home.

Sounds like a lot of fun, but in a heavily loaded open cockpit airplane, the romance wears off after day 2, and it becomes an exercise in patience and perseverance. But we were committed, so by golly we were going to have fun!

Our first weather briefing revealed that the Tehachapi Pass was socked in, so we cooled our heels in the airport terminal for a while. Can't be that bad, we thought, so we decided to go take a look. We launched, and headed for the Pass. We didn't go far before we saw that the reports were accurate. The ceilings were so low we had no choice. Back to the airport we went, and back to the hotel.

The next morning, the weather had improved. Not a drastic improvement, but enough that we decided to try again. We loaded the plane, took off in blue skies, and turned toward the Pass. You could see there was now some breathing room beneath the cloud layer, which covered only the Pass itself. We could see that the Mojave was clear, and the tops were low enough that we easily climbed above them. We crossed through the Pass eastbound over a beautiful white layer of cotton.

Conscious of the mountains to either side of us, I kept us directly over the highway, which I could see on the portable GPS hanging around my neck on a lanyard. The Stearman had sufficient instruments (what is called a "partial panel") that I knew if the engine tanked while over the Pass, I could glide straight ahead and descend through the clouds, which wouldn't take long. According to the weather briefer on the phone, I'd break out with about 500' to spare. Just enough to deadstick down and land between the cars. Not pretty, but as a backup plan, it made me feel better. And the engine had run perfectly for long enough by then that we were beginning to have a modicum of faith in it.

We were only over the Pass for a short while, and soon the Mojave Desert lay before us in all its desolate beauty. We could see the huge military runway off to our left as we inched our way to our next stop, Barstow.

Conscious of our goal of making Winslow by sunset, we made the stop as short as possible, and were soon airborne again, heading for Kingman. The desert environment was to be our on-again-off-again scenery for the next 5 days. One would think we would encounter at least occasionally moderate temperatures in the desert, but we spent about 5 days flying through the western half of the United States, and the only use we got out of short-sleeved shirts was as undergarments. From the time we entered the desert until the time we arrived in Minnesota, we both wore basically every stitch of outer clothing (everything except socks and underwear) we packed. Even with multiple layers of shirts, a sweatshirt, a full flight suit, a leather flying jacket, and a parachute on my back, I was cold. Early morning takeoffs were usually in the low 30s, and we would immediately climb to a cruising altitude that was 5-10 degrees colder yet. Shivering through the last half of each leg, we'd park by the gas pumps and then run inside to sit with a hot cup of coffee until we once again had to hit the road 20 minutes later.

The trip went more or less as planned, except for an extra night in Winslow, spent seeking medical attention for severe sunburn. I won't go into that, except to advise you to never fly across the high desert in the back cockpit of an open cockpit airplane, wearing no sunscreen on your face. To make it an even worse decision, I had ignored the warning on an antibiotic I had been taking for a recent bout of food poisoning I had encountered in Asia on my day job. "Stay out of the sun while taking this medication," it advised, but I ignored that and headed for the high desert in an open cockpit. Smart, huh?

So, for the rest of the trip, I looked like a hockey goalie, with several layers of prescription sunscreen and Silvadeen on my face. Duly penitent for my poor health planning, we launched from Winslow early in the cold morning, and the rest of the trip is a fairly uneventful series of gas stops and overnights. The weather stayed sunny and pleasant, albeit cold, all the way to Minnesota. Great people at all the stops, without exception, and wonderful sightseeing. You've never seen a cattle yard until you've flown over it in an open cockpit airplane at 500' with the cows turning to look up at you, and the unmistakable smell of manure filling the air swirling around you. It's like being a pilot and a rancher all at once. Woohoo, ride 'em cowboy!

After a week in the air, we crossed from Iowa into Minnesota, almost home. Still cold, but now happy, I rolled the wheels onto the grass runway at my home base, Faribault, Minnesota. I taxied to my hangar, and was met there by several friends who heard the distinct sound of my radial engine. As we prepared to roll the plane into the hangar, I turned to dad, and said "Wow. I've never been that cold for that long in my life."

He smiled. "You can say that again."

I laughed. "This is one trip that will be a wonderful memory in the rear view mirror, but right now I just want to put the plane away, go get something hot to eat and drink, and not come out here again until the temp is above 70."

"You got that right."

As we put it away, my friends drifted over one at a time, with two comments: "Welcome home, nice plane!" followed after a minute or two by "What happened to your face?" Happy to tell of the airborne adventure, but pained and embarrassed to tell of the sunburn, I related the whole week's adventure several times.

It was good to be home, good to have another Stearman, and good to have had another in a series of aerial adventures with my father.

I owned that Stearman for several years. It was even more fun when I could pick my sunny warm days for aviating, instead of having to take off into cold mornings as Dad and I had to do on the trip home. I gave many people biplane rides, went to many pancake breakfasts, and did some basic aerobatics now and then. Sometimes I would just go out to the hangar and sit with a beverage and enjoy being with the plane. At times like that it was easy to once again be that 7 year old boy in the right seat of his parents' car, watching spellbound as that old yellow Stearman flew by. There's nothing quite like fulfilling a promise to yourself that you made in your youth.

Airplane #17: 1961 Piper PA-18 N3785Z

Another airplane type that had always caught my eye was the Piper PA-18 Super Cub. I had owned and flown two Piper J-3s by that time, and they were lots of fun, but there was a mystique about the Super Cub that I yearned to experience. I had always visited the Super Cub listings in Trade-A-Plane and Barnstormers, and wistfully looked at the ones for sale. One day in early 2008, I found a PA-18 for sale in Texas. Hmmm, I thought. It might be time for a road trip…

A phone call introduced me to the owner, McHayden Dillard. Yes, he still had it. Could I see it? Of course.

This was a good time to visit old friends of mine from Ann Arbor, Bill and Mary Trusler, who now lived in Texas, not far from the Super Cub. The next thing I knew I was in a car with Bill, on my way to look at the Cub. It looked OK, not perfect, but it was priced accordingly. I flew it, and we struck a deal. Before I knew it, on April 28, 2008, I was leaving from McHayden's ranch airstrip, northbound with my "new" Super Cub.

After stops in Terrel, TX, Muskogee, OK, Joplin, MO, Lexington, MO, and Perry, IA, I arrived back at home base in Faribault, MN. The plane fit in my hangar with the Stearman, although it was a bit tight. No matter, I had my Super Cub!

I flew that Cub for almost a year, and sold it in April, 2009. I reluctantly admitted I was no longer a young man (a fact that gets more true with each passing year...), and the PA-18 was just too hard for me to get in and out of, so I moved it along to a rancher who needed it. The Super Cub itch having been scratched, I was ready for the next adventure.

Airplane #18 - 2006 American Champion 8KCAB Decathlon N24BY

Okay, so my aging frame didn't want to do the gymnastics required to get into Cubs anymore. By this time the Stearman had been sold, and I still wanted a plane to fly year round. What was I to do about that? My good friend, Bob Peasley, had what looked to me like a great solution: a 2006 American Champion 8KCAB Super Decathlon. It was much easier to get in and out of than the Super Cub, plus had a 180hp Lycoming engine with a constant speed prop, a real hot rod. I decided I had to have a Decathlon of my very own.

So, back to Trade-Plane and Barnstormers I went. Most Citabrias and Decathlons were pricey. Descended from the iconic Aeronca Champ of the 1940s, they offered decent speed, the mystique of a tail dragger, and true fully aerobatic capabilities. I decided to concentrate my search on the more recent models. They were, of course, more expensive than their older siblings, but for once I decided to treat myself. I was tired of constantly fixing worn out old airplanes.

Even newer Decathlons had seen hard aerobatic use, however, so one had to be careful. Obvious signs of mistreatment could occasionally be found, so it paid to look a prospect over in detail. One of the problems I encountered over and over as I looked was cracked paint. The American Champion factory had chosen to paint their entire line of products with a type of paint that was quite shiny, and looked great for years with very little maintenance. The "wet look." But what I found on almost every Decathlon that was more than a couple years old were cracks in the paint, usually 1-4 inches long, but some as much as a foot long. You couldn't see them until you got up close, but they were there, and they ruined that "new car smell," as far as I was concerned. My theory is that they arose from the unfortunate decision to apply a finish coat that was a completely different type of compound than the dope over which it was applied, and it obviously tended to crack when subjected to the wide range of temperatures to which an airplane is exposed. These airplanes were exposed to paint-cracking temps at altitude on many flights. Add to that the fabric flexing that results from flight, especially aerobatic flight, and you have a recipe for cracking. Look at the finish on most other aerobatic planes painted with a different enamel or dope, and you generally won't find cracks. Look at any Decathlon with factory paint that's more than a few years old, and you will find them.

It was a frustrating search. The sellers, of course, always said their planes were subjected to only occasional light aerobatics, but the signs were there in the logbooks and on the paint that they had been "rode hard and put away wet." I didn't blame anyone for using the plane the way it had been designed, but on the other hand I wanted as pristine an example as I could find.

After many phone calls and several frustrating trips, I finally found one that sounded promising in Texas. It was a 2006 Decathlon, just like my friend Bob's 2006 model. I mean JUST like it, right down to the paint job. The two planes had serial numbers only 15 numbers apart. After I called Bob and asked if he'd mind having the "sister ship" to his plane based on the same airport (he said it would actually be fun), I made plans to go see it.

It was at Pearland, a small airport on the south edge of Houston. Aha! Houston, where Bill and Mary Trusler lived! I saw this as another reason to make the trip, as it gave me a great excuse for a visit. Having just been there when buying the Super Cub, the jokes started immediately about how every time I needed a plane I'd head for Bill and Mary's, and I guess I didn't mind. I hope they didn't either.

The Decathlon was more than I could have hoped for. It had obviously seen very light use, and the warm Texas temps coupled with light aerobatic use resulted in a finish that was virtually crack-free. Inside and out, everywhere I looked, the plane was pristine. A short negotiation resulted in my leaving Texas as a new Decathlon owner.

I went home to arrange the transfer of funds, etc., and get a complete Decathlon checkout from Bob Peasley in the sister ship to the one I just bought. I returned to Texas a week later to retrieve my prize.

One final visit to Bill and Mary, which included Bill taking my new ship for a ride (he also was a Decathlon owner), a promise to come back the next time I was airplane shopping (we all had a good laugh about that), and I was northbound with my like-new Super Decathlon.

The plane ran as well as it looked on the trip. I have nothing but pleasant memories of what was becoming familiar terrain on the route which I had just flown a couple of years before with the Super Cub. The difference was that this time the trip went much faster, as a Decathlon is a quicker ship than a Cub. Much quicker. And quieter. And less windy than the just-barely-closed-cockpit Super Cub.

Since the Super D was so fast, I began using it to visit my parents and brother in Poplar Grove, IL. I convinced Peggy to go along, since it cut the transit time to less than half of what it was in the car for those visits. Peggy even showed some interest in what was going on around us in the plane, and she went on several of those trips.

It began to bother me, though, that if anything happened to me en route like a heart attack, she would have considerable difficulty getting a Decathlon back on the ground in one piece without my help. She agreed, and since the Super D was obviously being used more for the Poplar Grove visits than for anything else, we discussed getting a go-somewhere airplane that would be more user-friendly for her, should she ever have to land it herself.

On top of everything else, she did not like sitting behind me, where we could not communicate visually. The Super D had a very nice intercom, and with good headsets it allowed free conversation, but she said she felt isolated back there. And I did not feel comfortable flying from the back, since my view of the instruments was very limited, and I could not reach the GPS, communications radio, etc., from the rear seat.

In short, I had to admit the Super D was a great choice for me when I flew alone, but if I wanted to take Peggy with me on trips, it was not such a good plane. The natural choice was a Cessna 172 or 182, two of the easiest airplanes to land ever produced. In a real emergency, all a neophyte would have to do is get one of those two planes within a few of the runway at anywhere near the right speed, chop the throttle, try to keep it on the centerline, hope for the best, and they'd stand a good chance of walking away. The plane might be bent, but they'd be alive. Okay, that's an oversimplification, but let's just say a 172 or 182 is a HECK of a lot easier to land than a Super Decathlon.

Encouraged by her enthusiasm, I decided to move the Super D along to someone who wanted an airplane for sport aerobatics.

I approached Roy Redman of Rare Aircraft about selling it for me, as they were an American Champion dealer. He said he'd be glad to help. I wasn't sure how efficient they'd really be in reaching the market, but I knew I didn't really want to jump into the project of selling it. I had already mentally shifted into the Cessna 172/182 shopping mode.

It was not long before Roy told me he'd taken a deposit on the plane. They were well worth their sales commission, as I didn't have to do a thing except provide the plane and take the money. The Super Decathlon was soon on its way to a happy new owner, and I was already trolling the 172s and 182s for sale online.

Airplane # 19 - 1967 Cessna 182K
N47KS

I didn't know how frustrating this search was to be. Cessna made about a gazillion 172s and 182s, and one would first think that was an advantage to a prospective buyer. The reality, however, was that there were so many of them out there, each with its own individual equipment, maintenance, use, damage, and storage history, that the project was overwhelming. I had to limit the search somehow.

I started by calling various sellers around the country and asking questions. I was by no means an inexperienced buyer, and it wasn't too hard to figure out that even though there were many 172s and 182s out there, the really good ones had either sold by the time I called (usually within 72 hours of their being listed), or the reason they hadn't sold was that they were overpriced by as much as 40-50% over book retail. I wasn't about to go on a cross-country buying trip to look at a deal that was obviously flawed due to price.

Unfortunately, misrepresented airplanes were common. It was pretty normal for a seller to describe his airplane as "pristine, on a scale from 1 to 10, it's an 11..." Then after I'd traveled across the country on a 2 day trip to look at it, I'd discover on that 1-to-10 scale, it was actually about a 4. I recall one seller describing his 182 as having no damage history, so I went to look. He was right to the extent that the aircraft records SHOWED no damage repairs, but that was because they had obviously just "fixed" major damage and not entered the accident repair in the logs. Or maybe all the logbooks weren't there! It was obvious by looking at the wrinkled fuselage skin and botched riveting on the "repair" that it had been fixed after dark in someone's hangar, probably by a "mechanic" who didn't know what he was doing.

It was obvious to me that I was either going to have to overpay for a good plane, or be so "on top of the market" that I'd be the first to respond to a new ad. The other alternative was to look at airplanes that weren't yet for sale, and simply ask the owner if they had thought about selling their nice 172 or 182, and if so please call me. This, as it turned out, was how I found my 182.

I had made a trip to Park Rapids, MN, to look at a 182 that didn't fit my requirements, but while I was there, the dealer casually mentioned that there was another 182 on the airport that wasn't actually for sale, but he knew the owner "was thinking about it." He had a key to hangar, and showed me the not-yet-for-sale 1967 182K Skylane. It was well equipped, IFR, with an S-TEC 60 autopilot, etc., and a beautiful fairly fresh professional paint job. I left my name and phone number with the dealer, asking him to call if the owner decided to sell.

It didn't take long. After a few days, the dealer called me, and I was on my way back to Park Rapids to take a closer look at the plane. I gave them a deposit, contingent on the plane passing a fresh annual inspection at their cost. Also, I had not even run it yet and I wanted to do that before I closed the deal. They had been a little suspect of the engine, as it had not been run in about 8 months, so instead of taxiing it to the shop to clean it up for the agreed-upon fresh annual inspection, they towed it over, and decided to open it up and take a look at the lifters and camshaft before trying to start it. Good call.

I was there when they opened the engine up for a look, and they found that the lifters and camshaft were pitted from the time in storage. I said, of course, that I couldn't take the plane like that, and they agreed. Instead of calling the deal off, we reached a compromise: the engine would come completely apart, inspected for further corrosion, and reassembled with all new lifters, new gaskets, and a brand new camshaft, at the seller's cost. The big drawback to this plan was the time it would take to accomplish all of that, and of course I was anxious to fly. We pressed on, and about a month later I returned to fly, pay for, and pick up my new/old Cessna 182 Skylane.

Peggy and I really enjoyed that plane. We took many trips in it, most of them to Poplar Grove to visit my family. We would roll it right into my brother's hangar, with Peggy still seated in the cockpit if it was cold or windy, and she would step out once it was inside. Since Jim's hangar was attached to his house, she was about 50' from the comfort of Jim and Colleen's home. When it was time to depart several days later, if the weather was cool or breezy, she could once again climb into the cockpit in the heated hangar before we rolled the plane out. She felt pampered!

We also took that plane to Ann Arbor. After moving to Minnesota, we had always missed Ann Arbor, and returned regularly to visit favorite old places and friends, but had taken the airline on those trips. Doing it with our own plane gave those visits an entirely new, relaxed character. We were able to run our own schedule, and arrive and depart at our leisure. In addition, the hangar space we found to rent on a nightly basis for the short duration of the visit was directly across the taxiway from my old T-hangar that I had rented for many years, in which I had kept my airplanes when we had lived there (airplanes #6 through #12). It was a real trip down memory lane.

One of the main reasons we had switched from the Decathlon to the Skylane was so we could have a plane that Peg could learn to land. She initially showed some interest in that, but as the months passed and we took several trips in the 182, I could see that Peggy was more interested in just "getting there," rather than actually doing any flying. I offered to pay for an instructor to teach her, and even though she thought that might be "okay," she never brought it up unless I did. I could see her heart was not going to be in it, so I didn't push it.

I saw the same scenario developing that occurred after I had owned the Cessna 140, airplane #15, for a while. I would go to the hangar, putter around for an hour or so, then go home. Peggy would ask how the plane was, and I would answer, "It's okay, I guess."

She'd say "why just 'okay'? This is your hobby, the thing that's supposed to really blow your skirt up."

"I know, and I do like it, but the 182 is really for 'going somewhere,' not purely for fun."

"What would it take to make your hobby fun again?" I knew where this was headed.

"I miss the Stearman…"

"Okay, we've gone this route before, and I feel the same way I did then. Life is short, and there are no guarantees about how much or how little time any of us has left. If a Stearman is what will make you happy, it is what you should have."

"We'd have to sell the 182."

"So what?"

"We'd have to go back to driving to Poplar Grove."

"We've done that many times, we can easily do it again. Put the 182 on the market, take the money, and go Stearman shopping." Once again, music to my ears!

One nice thing about Cessna 182s is the fact that there will always be a strong market for them, if they're well taken care of and priced properly. Mine was definitely well cared for, and I decided to not be greedy on the price. I asked a price above wholesale but below book retail, and advertised it online.

The phone started ringing (like, in about an hour), and soon the plane sold to a very nice fellow who lived not far from where we lived in Minnesota. It had been fun owning a Skylane, but nowhere near as much fun as owning a Stearman. I was looking forward to the search!

Airplane # 20 - 1941 Boeing A75N1 Stearman N985

So, back to the Stearman market. I remembered the drawbacks from my previous experiences Stearman shopping. In such a limited market, even the good ones that are reasonably priced sometimes take a while to sell. After all, you are looking at an airplane that exists for one reason and one reason only: it's a pure and simple toy. At any given moment, each Stearman out there has only a few potentially serious buyers, and everyone else is just a tire kicker or dreamer (not that there's anything wrong with dreaming, I do it all the time!).

As I reentered the market as a buyer with cash, I knew that I had the advantage, so decided to be picky. I was in my mid sixties, so while not yet an official "geezer," I realized I had a limited number of years left to enjoy whatever plane I chose. I didn't want a fixer-upper or a hangar queen, but rather was looking for as nearly a perfect example of a restored stock Stearman as I could find on the used market. Not knowing how many more years I was going to be able to take that big yard-high step up to the lower wing, I wanted to spend that time flying, not repairing a worn out machine. This allowed me to quickly narrow the search. I decided to eliminate anything that had been last restored more than 10 years previously, and would only go look at ones that were advertised as being close to perfect.

It was obvious that there were only going to be a few possibilities that fit my requirements. I also arbitrarily decided to look only for Stearmans that were finished in stock military configuration and livery, and eliminated the ones with "big engines." The 220hp Continental or 225hp Lycoming engines underpowered the Stearman, but they were authentic, and the antique appeal was what I enjoyed.

There were only a couple planes that fit all my requirements. I called on the closest one first, as it was only about 500 miles away, in southern Indiana, and found myself talking to a fine gentleman, Doctor Bill Nice.

"Do you still have the Stearman for sale?"

"Yes, I do."

"What can you tell me about it?"

"It was restored about 6 years ago, and is pretty close to perfect. It is a trophy winner, having been awarded the 'Best PT-17' at Galesburg last Fall." Galesburg is the official yearly fly-in convention of the Stearman Restorers Association. Winning an award there was significant. I needed to know more.

"Who did the restoration?" This is where a lot of planes can be eliminated, as their last restorations were cosmetic only.

Dr. Nice answered, "It was done by Scott White. I had him take it down to bare bones and build it back to better than new."

Now Bill really had my full attention. Scott White had an impeccable reputation as a meticulous restorer of trophy winning Stearmans, one of the best in the country. I was hooked, and said "Well, I think I better see it in person."

We traded information about schedules, and Bill said if I could go to the Bloomington, Indiana airport, he'd meet me at his hangar, where the plane was. I checked the airline schedules from Minneapolis to Indianapolis, and found a flight that left the next day. It had seats open (a big advantage when you are traveling space available!), so away I went. After arriving at the Indianapolis airport, I rented a car and soon I was at Bill's hangar in Bloomington.

The airport manager let me in while I waited for Bill, and I turned on the lights. There sat the most immaculately restored Stearman I had ever seen. I had some time alone with the plane now, and crawled over it, carefully removing inspection panels and opening cowlings, looking deeply into the plane's innards with a flashlight and mirror. The more time I spent, the more excited I got. Each place I looked was more perfect than the last. Bill showed up, and we talked.

The asking price was actually not that bad for this plane, but it needed to have a Mode C transponder installed because my home airport is very near MSP Class B airspace. That would cost me about $5,000 to have that done, so I asked if there was any wiggle room on the price. He said a little, but not much. I made an offer, but he was definite that even his asking price was way under what he had invested in the plane. I told him I'd sleep on it.

I called Peggy, and briefed her on the plane. I told her I'd just seen the most beautiful Stearman ever.

She said, "Well it sounds like you've found your new plane!"

"Not so fast," I said. "His asking price would be worth it if it had a transponder, which it doesn't"

"How much would it cost to put one in?"

"About $5,000. I made him an offer, and I think he was a little upset. I told him I'd think about it."

"Is it really as nice as you say?"

"Better."

"You want my opinion?"

"Of course."

"Are you NUTS? You know how hard it is to find a good airplane. You're still young and healthy enough to enjoy this, and it's the type of plane you want. Pay the nice man his money, and start making plans to bring it home!"

What a gal. I thought for a minute. "You're right. I better hang up, I've got to go make a phone call…"

I called Bill and told him about the conversation with Peggy, and said we've got a deal. He chuckled and said of Peggy, "I really like that lady. You're very lucky." He was right about that!

I immediately began to make plans for bringing the Stearman home. The distance from Indiana to

Minnesota is not great for a Stearman, but there was still snow on the ground and open cockpit flying requires a certain Viking personality in cold weather.

I did all the non-flying details first, getting insurance arranged, money in place, etc. It also occurred to me that it had now been a couple of years since I had last flown a tail dragger. Time to once again call Bob Peasley. As I said, Bob is also a retired airline pilot, and a born instructor. He enjoys teaching in airplanes, and helping keep people safe and sharp.

He also still owned the Super Decathlon that was the mate to my old Super D. I told him of my concerns about climbing back in a Stearman after a couple of years of flying nose wheel airplanes, and he offered to take me up for a workout.

And what a workout it was! Two different airports, several different runways, all hard surface, some with winds right down the runway, others with direct crosswinds of up to 15 knots. I started getting tired, but I think Bob was enjoying himself because he didn't want to quit.

I had a great time, and by the time we parked the Super D and got out, Bob and I both felt I was ready to once again get in a Stearman. I was ready to bring back N985. All my cold weather flying clothes, overnight kit, and tools were packed, so then I was just waiting for light winds, VFR weather and temps above 40 degrees.

It turned out to be a long wait. The need for VFR weather actually works against the desire for moderate temps in the Midwest in the spring. The best weather comes with an approaching high-pressure area, and with the clockwise flow surrounding a high, it also means falling temps. So, you usually have to choose between low clouds and high temps or high clouds and low temps. I decided the ceilings and visibilities were more important, so after waiting several weeks I saw an approaching high and headed for Indiana.

The next morning dawned clear, with light winds, but cold. Not to be deterred, I went to the airport and donned my long underwear, sweatshirt, flying suit, and leather jacket. The plane was in a heated hangar, so I waited to wheel it out until I was ready to fire up and go. After all loading was complete and the preflight inspection done, I opened the door, rolled it out with the help of a local line attendant, and climbed in.

I could hardly move, I had so many clothes on, but I managed to strap in, run through the starting procedure, and hit the starter. The moment of truth had come, as I had not even heard the engine run prior to this point, believing that any plane as sharp as this one MUST be okay mechanically. I was not disappointed, as the 220 Continental roared to life after about two revolutions.

Much relieved to be in motion with my new prize, I listened to the ATIS and taxied to the runway. Extremely happy that I had spent the day with Bob Peasley in his Super D blowing the cobwebs off my rusty tail dragger skills, I took a look down the runway to make sure there was nothing in my path, and fed the throttle in to the stop. Tail up, dance on the rudder, ease the stick back, and I was airborne!

Two things were immediately obvious: the engine was fine, and the airplane was rigged correctly. I turned to the heading I had determined would put me approximately on course, and climbed to an altitude that would clear all obstacles in my path. I was on my way home, ready for whatever the future held for me, and this Stearman.

The first fuel stop was Pontiac, Illinois. I was cold, but anxious to keep moving while I had the weather. I ran inside to visit the men's room, paid for the gas, and returned to the plane, anxious to hear that 220 roar again. But wait, what's this? My heart sank as I saw the puddle of oil beneath the cowling. Hoping fervently that it was from the last plane to have parked there, I opened the left cheek cowl. What I found was hot engine oil coming from the back of the accessory case draining to the bottom of the lower cowl and pooling on the concrete below. I had been there only about twenty minutes, and the puddle was about a foot in diameter.

I went in to see if there was a mechanic on duty, and my luck was holding. Not only was the FBO there, he was a mechanic who had an extensive history of working on crop dusters with radial engines. He quickly pegged the problem as a leaking hose on the oil pressure fitting, and proceeded to wipe it clean and reseat the hose. He had me ready to go in an hour or so. When I asked him what I owed him, he just smiled and said "no charge!" Ahh, small airports, small towns. It is indeed a brotherhood.

I had been there long enough for the winds to come up a bit, but I decided I better try for one more leg. Back into all my layers of clothes, I hit the starter, and away I went. I made it as far as Whiteside County Airport, Illinois, where it became obvious as I entered the traffic pattern how cold and tired I had become. It had not only been a long day, but a stressful one. Cautioning myself to be extra careful, I made a not-too-pretty landing and taxied in to the ramp.

The fellows working at the FBO were very helpful in getting the plane inside a hangar for the evening. I arranged for a hotel for the night, and as soon as I was alone with the Stearman, with no one watching, I tried to look inconspicuous as I grabbed a rag and flashlight and went to check the status of the oil leak. I was encouraged that this time there was no telltale dripping from the cowling, and held my breath as I opened the left cheek cowl. I peered inside, and much to my relief it appeared dry! A more careful check with a clean rag revealed no apparent leakage, so I headed for the hotel.

After a good night's sleep, I headed for the airport bright and early. The weather again looked clear but cold, so I gritted my teeth and headed north to Minnesota.

Those cool temperatures were starting to get to me. I had been in the air for about 5 minutes when I began to feel REALLY cold. "Press on," I kept telling myself. "You made the choice that VFR weather was worth the cold, so suck it up, Nancy." It's easy to engage in bravado when you're flight planning in a warm hotel or FBO, but another thing entirely when you are wearing 40 pounds of clothes and still shivering.

Flying an open cockpit plane on a short hop is a completely different activity from actually going somewhere in one. It's difficult to read a GPS and navigate, while keeping the plane right side up. Map reading is an art in itself, requiring a strategic method of folding the chart, so as to minimize having to open the chart in flight. The ideal fold will allow you see the entire leg at once, without having to do more than open one fold and flip the chart over. And, of course, the wind is ready to take that carefully prepared map and snatch it from your hands as soon as you let your guard down. I have lost several such charts to the slipstream over the years. If I am flying a route with which I am really unfamiliar, I will occasionally take a duplicate chart along and sit on it, so I have a spare in reserve for that eventuality.

The other negative about flying cross country in an open cockpit biplane is the fatigue that results from the wind. It's hard to describe, but the wind just takes a toll on you. After a full day of the wind beating on your helmet, shaking your sunglasses and blowing into every open flap in your clothes, it begins to affect the clarity of your thought. And, of course, the noise and vibration from the big radial engine don't help. It's fun, but can be very tiring.

Frozen to the bone, I saw my home field of Faribault, Minnesota finally creep into sight. The last 10 miles seemed like a hundred, but I finally rolled the wheels on the runway and taxied to the hangar. I sat for a moment, so cold I could hardly move. Home once again.

That Stearman was the nicest Stearman I had ever owned, and I was to have many wonderful flights in it. Two round trips to the National Stearman fly in at Galesburg, Illinois, provided many great memories and a few not-so-great ones (like the night I cowered in the hotel in Galesburg while a monster thunderstorm ravaged the area...). On one of those trips, the plane won the fly-in award (again) for Best Army Stearman; the second time in 3 years that plane had won the award at Galesburg. It was a real compliment to the gentleman who had done the restoration, Scott White.

We had many wonderful hangar barbecues with the Stearman, and my daughter Catherine Sheppard (who is a professional fashion stylist) even did a fashion blog photo shoot with the plane as a backdrop. These 3 photos were taken by her husband, Ian, and are from that shoot. Catherine is the model:

Our other daughter Christine Cecil and her husband Robby, together with me in the photo below, also have been frequent attendees at our infamous hangar barbecues. Everyone loves that Stearman, not to mention the barbecues at the end of the flying day!

Airplane #21 -1993 American General AG5B Tiger N155E

It should be obvious by now that whenever I own a pure fun airplane, I miss the ability to travel somewhere fast, and vice versa. Not bored with the Stearman (never!), I nevertheless once again craved the ability to get in a plane and fly somewhere quickly and efficiently, in my shirtsleeves, with my sunglasses sedately perched on my nose in a total absence of cockpit wind. I was totally happy with the Stearman for fun flying on summer days, but was once again beginning to tire of the excessive amounts of driving necessary to go visit my family in Poplar Grove, Illinois. I had mentioned this to my brother Jim on several of those visits, bemoaning the fact that the Stearman was fun, but not a good plane for trips. Jim had a Grumman Tiger that he used to go places, and I remarked to him that I bet it would fit in the hangar with my Stearman. He allowed as to how it probably would do that, and I mentioned to him that should he ever decide to sell it, that he should give me a call.

Big mistake.

Jim's airplane preferences ran more along the lines of IFR equipped high tech, high speed planes full of bells and whistles. His Grumman met those desires in a basic way, but he wanted to go to the next level: a Cirrus. The Cirrus was a serious go-somewhere machine that made the Grumman look more like the Wright Flyer. Full of the latest computer technology, composite construction, and a full-aircraft recovery parachute for emergencies, the Cirrus was worth more than twice what the Grumman was, even used. So when he called and told me he had put a deposit on a used Cirrus, and wanted now to sell the Grumman, it was time for me to put my money where my mouth was.

Jim's plane was technically a 1993 American General AG5B Tiger. It was one of the last Tigers made by American General, and was a type in high demand in a niche community of flyers. I had ridden in his Grumman on many occasions, and found it appealing as a cross country ship that would allow Peg and me to easily visit our relatives in Poplar Grove. I told him I'd take it, and we agreed on a price that was fair for both of us. The Tiger was soon mine.

Jim came and picked me up at Faribault in the Tiger, and I flew him back home in it as he did a very complete checkout in the plane for me. I was delighted to once again have a go-somewhere plane that allowed me the luxury of traveling to Midwest destinations like Poplar Grove and Ann Arbor in a fast, fun fashion.

This plane was equipped for instrument flight, meaning I could file IFR flight plans and legally go cross country in the clouds, subject to the limitations of avoiding icing, convective activity (thunderstorms, even small ones), night flight, or very low ceilings and visibilities. I got my instrument currency back, and could now file IFR to destinations.

Even though the Tiger fit in my hangar along with the Stearman, it was fairly crowded in there. In the summer the biplane was my aircraft of preference, and so was the one I usually put in front. Any time I wanted to fly the Grumman, I had to play "musical airplanes." This made flying the Tiger labor intensive, and so I soon decided to rent an additional hangar from the city for the Tiger.

The situation lasted for two years, during which time I used the Tiger about once a month. Most often, we used it for trips to Poplar Grove to visit family. Age takes its toll on all of us, and my parents were no exception. My mother had developed Alzheimer's disease, and my father's time was increasingly devoted to her care. His hangar was not used nearly as much for his aviation hobby, which made it available for the Tiger during my visits, making the Tiger an even more convenient way for Peggy and me to visit.

Still, owning and maintaining two airplanes was a very expensive proposition, both in time and dollars. It became obvious this time, as it had several times before, how quickly the daily chores and costs drain your resources. Since I could only fly one at a time, and the Tiger saw the light of day only about a dozen times a year, I once again decided to concentrate on the real love of my aviation hobby, the Stearman. I put the Tiger on the market, through a dealer who specialized in that type of plane. After a few months, it sold, and I was now down to the plane to which I had repeatedly returned after 50 years of flying: the Stearman.

Some final thoughts

Airplanes have always been close by in my life. I'd like to say there was a Grand Plan in their choice and order of appearance, but the truth is that they were there basically because it made me happy to own them. They were fun. They were like magic carpets that always made me smile. I knew from my earliest years that I was destined to be a pilot, and the appearance of the Taylorcraft in my life when I was fifteen was inevitable.

It's all a matter of following your dreams. As I write the closing chapter of this memoir, I am 69 years old, and have been retired from airline flying for just over 9 years. I am not retired, not yet anyway, from general aviation. Even though I can't deny the first signs of aging, I can only hope that that there are more chapters to come. Dad flew until he was almost 90, and my mother lived to 94, so if my general health cooperates, I trust I have several adventures, and maybe airplanes, left in my future.

I was driving to my hangar in Faribault recently, on my way to work on whatever the project of the day was, and it occurred to me how often I go out there. I go several times a week to fly, or to work on the plane, or just to have lunch and putter around. The point is simply to just be there, to be around the things that have always drawn me like a magnet. My toys. It's like I was saying to Peggy just the other day: I never feel more alive than when I am out there.

I've still got Airplane #20, my beloved Stearman, and when I open the hangar door and step inside, my heart beats a bit faster, and the little kid inside me stirs. He looks at the gorgeous machine in front of him, and smiles. He speaks from a time 60 years ago, from the back seat of my parents' car:

"Hey, it's a Stearman!"

About the Author

John F. Hanson was born in Madison, Wisconsin in 1947. He was raised in Ann Arbor, Michigan, where he attended public schools. He attended the University of Michigan, where he studied Aerospace Engineering. While an undergraduate at the university, he built his flying time as a flight instructor and charter pilot. At the conclusion of his college junior year, at the age of twenty, he was offered and accepted a position as pilot for North Central Airlines. He continued his college education at the University of Michigan part time while he flew as an airline pilot, first finishing his BSE in Aerospace Engineering. He then was admitted to graduate school at Michigan, again attending part time for 3 ½ years, eventually obtaining his MSE in Aerospace.

His airline career lasted almost 40 years, and included (through mergers) flying under the airline banners first of North Central Airlines, then Republic Airlines, and finally retiring from Northwest Airlines as a captain on the Boeing 747-400. He was the very bottom pilot on the seniority list at North Central on his hire date in 1968, and over the next 39 ½ years gradually rose to the very top of the seniority list at Northwest Airlines. He spent 13 months as #1 before he eventually retired on October 29, 2007.

He now enjoys his time flying his beloved Stearman on sunny days.

Made in the USA
Las Vegas, NV
31 May 2021

23970340R00100